# Chefs

# Eat

A PRO'S GUIDE TO
REINVENTING YOUR
SANDWICH GAME.

# Melts

# Too.

DARREN
PURCHESE

**hardie grant** books

## Start.
### 01–25

## Press.
### 26–55

## Grill.
### 56–81

This book uses 15 ml (½ fl oz) tablespoons; cooks with 20 ml (¾ fl oz) tablespoons should be scant with their tablespoon measurements.

It also uses metric cup measurements, i.e. 250 ml for 1 cup; in the US a cup is 8 fl oz, just smaller, and American cooks should be generous in their cup measurements; in the UK a cup is 10 fl oz and British cooks should be scant with their cup measurements.

# A word from Shannon Bennett.

It was a proud moment when Darren asked me to consider writing a few comments about his wonderful new book on toasted sandwiches – for several reasons.

First of all he did not need to include the word 'consider'. It was my honour! – especially given this is a man who worked exceptionally hard early in both our careers as my head pastry chef. To this day many of Darren's recipes remain on my menus. Second, as a father of six children and partner to a busy professional, I need all the help I can get for great food ideas that are quick, inventive and tasty. This book has the lot.

Of the recipes I have sampled so far, the grilled sardines with romesco is up there with my favourites, but I have also found much inspiration from Darren's words and ideas. For example, the taleggio flatbreads with mozzarella, prosciutto and basil momentarily transformed my kids from incoherent minions on full power to quiet, content connoisseurs – they even asked for seconds! Temperatures were taken and strong words exchanged, debating whether they were all medically OK. Why were they so enamoured with their lunch? Answers were varied and none made sense, but I must assume they all loved the speedy delivery time and the way the filling and the bread became one. I was crowned the Toastie King for all of 30 minutes, which was then completely forgotten when the missus decided to give the apple and blackberry jaffle a crack. She has held onto the crown since. Darren, thank you for my 30 minutes of glory.

Recipes aside, congratulations on a truly great book, which I know will appeal to so many different people, and bring much pleasure.

SHANNON BENNETT

# Why melts?

I love toast. I know I'm not the only one. There's nothing better than hot toast with a thick layer of melting butter threatening to dribble down your arm, or bubbling melted cheese on a slice of your favourite bread. Everyone loves a melt and has a favourite recipe. The great thing about melts is that anyone can create one. Mention melts to someone and they'll tell you about their signature recipe. When my friends and colleagues heard about this book they all said, 'That's a great idea, I love melts!'

I feel I was destined to write this book, as toast, cheese on toast and melts are my thing. If pastry and chocolate are my profession and passion, then melts are my hobby and obsession. In fact the first things I ever cooked were toasted creations, and my favourite foods always had melted cheese somewhere. When I was a kid, Mum used to make me simple white-bread cheese on toast. I loved it and would ask for more until I was able to make my own. From then on I was in heaven and would experiment with my own extra toppings, different cheeses and breads. I was obsessed with creating the best melted-cheese experience ever.

Being a professional chef I am often asked if I enjoy cooking at home – the answer is yes! I love to cook for my wife, friends and family. I always make things from scratch, and especially enjoy cooking food that I don't normally make in my day-to-day life. That doesn't mean that I'm always creating extravagantly complicated meals at home. I'm probably making the same things as you, and some of those things include melts. It's just that mine – whether savoury or sweet, with or without cheese – are possibly a bit more inventive and made with the same care as one of my elaborate sweet creations.

Over the years I have honed my cheese on toast to be the best it can be – but I'm not finished experimenting yet. Hopefully this book will open your eyes a little wider to the myriad possibilities for the humble melt. I hope this helps you lift your own melt game at home. Happy grilling!

DARREN

# Start.

(THINGS YOU'LL NEED)

# Harissa.

<u>Makes</u> 200 g (7 oz)

2 teaspoons cumin seeds
1 teaspoon coriander seeds
2 red capsicums (bell peppers),
   roasted and peeled
25 g (1 oz) bird's eye chillies,
   chopped (including seeds)
2 garlic cloves
salt flakes

**1/** Place the spices in a dry frying pan and toast them over a gentle heat, shaking the pan continuously to ensure the spices do not colour and burn. After 1–2 minutes, when their aroma is released, tip them into a mortar and pestle and grind them to a fine powder.

**2/** Transfer the powder to a food processor, add the remaining ingredients and blend to a smooth paste. The harissa will last for up to 1 week in the refrigerator, or you can freeze it in ice cube trays for up to 2 months – defrost a cube at a time, as needed.

# Tamari seeds.

<u>Makes</u> 300 g (10½ oz)

100 g (3½ oz) pepitas (pumpkin
   seeds)
100 g (3½ oz) sunflower seeds
40 g (1½ oz/¼ cup) pine nuts
40 g (1½ oz/¼ cup) sesame
   seeds
100 ml (3½ fl oz) tamari

**1/** Combine the seeds in a medium, clean, dry non-stick saucepan over medium heat. Move the seeds back and forth and toss to evenly toast them through, about 5 minutes. Once all the seeds have been evenly toasted to golden brown, remove the pan from the heat and add the tamari. Stir the seeds to ensure they are fully coated then leave the pan to cool.

**2/** Once cool, break the crunchy seed mix into small pieces with your hands and store them in a sealed container.

# Mayonnaise.

<u>Makes</u> 350 g (12½ oz)

3 egg yolks
1 tablespoon lemon juice
2 tablespoons warm water
salt flakes
250 ml (8½ fl oz/1 cup)
   canola oil

**1/** Combine the egg yolks, lemon juice, warm water and salt flakes in a tall, narrow measuring jug. Process well using a hand-held blender. Continue to blend while you add a tablespoon of oil to the jug. Mix until emulsified before slowly trickling in the remaining oil. Continue to blend in an up and down motion until you have a mayonnaise of the desired consistency.

# Vinaigrette.

Makes 175 ml (6 fl oz)

1 tablespoon balsamic vinegar
1 teaspoon dijon mustard
1 teaspoon wholegrain mustard
salt flakes
freshly ground black pepper
finely grated zest of ½ lemon
100 ml (3½ fl oz) light olive oil

**1/** Mix the vinegar with the mustards, salt, pepper and lemon zest. Slowly whisk in the oil to emulsify.

# Harissa vinaigrette.

Makes 200 ml (7 fl oz)

½ garlic clove
salt flakes
2 tablespoons Harissa
    (opposite page)
35 ml (1¼ fl oz) white-wine
    vinegar
125 ml (4 fl oz/½ cup) light
    olive oil
freshly ground black pepper

**1/** Crush the garlic with a pinch of salt using a mortar and pestle until very smooth, then stir in the harissa. Whisk in the vinegar followed by the oil and season with salt and pepper.

# Sweet mustard dressing.

Makes 250 ml (8½ fl oz/1 cup)

1 tablespoon dijon mustard
1 tablespoon wholegrain
    mustard
1 tablespoon English mustard
1 tablespoon white-wine vinegar
½ tablespoon caster (superfine)
    sugar
½ tablespoon chopped fresh dill
100 ml (3½ fl oz) olive oil

**1/** In a bowl, mix the mustards, vinegar, sugar and dill together well, then slowly whisk in the oil to emulsify.

# Thousand island dressing.

Makes 400 ml (13½ fl oz)

75 g (2¾ oz) Mayonnaise
(page 2), or use store-bought
Kewpie mayonnaise
2 tablespoons tomato sauce
(ketchup)
1 teaspoon dijon mustard
1 teaspoon of the pickling
vinegar from Dill pickles
(see page 9)
1 tablespoon finely chopped
French shallots
1 tablespoon finely chopped
cornichons
2 hard-boiled eggs, finely
chopped or grated

½ teaspoon smoked paprika
1 tablespoon finely chopped
fresh chives
1 teaspoon finely chopped
fresh dill
finely grated zest of ½ lemon
1 tablespoon finely chopped
roasted red capsicum
(bell pepper)
few drops of sriracha sauce
(see page 159) or other
hot chilli sauce
salt flakes
ground white pepper

1/ Make this dressing the day before serving if you can, to let the flavours develop. Place all the ingredients in a bowl and mix together gently with a spoon. Season to taste. Store in the refrigerator, covered, for up to 4 days.

# Yoghurt sauce.

Makes 450 g (1 lb)

400 g (14 oz) Greek-style
yoghurt
1 garlic clove, finely grated
finely grated zest of ½ lemon
1 tablespoon chopped fresh
flat-leaf (Italian) parsley
leaves
1 tablespoon chopped fresh
mint leaves
1 tablespoon chopped fresh dill
1 teaspoon white-wine vinegar
salt flakes
freshly ground black pepper

1/ Combine all the ingredients in a bowl. Keep in the refrigerator until needed.

# Chimichurri sauce.

**<u>Makes</u> 600 ml (20½ fl oz)**

*100 ml (3½ fl oz) sherry vinegar*
*100 ml (3½ fl oz) red-wine*
*vinegar*
*1 teaspoon salt flakes*
*½ red onion, finely diced*
*1 garlic bulb, cloves peeled*
*and finely grated*
*3 tablespoons finely chopped*
*fresh coriander (cilantro)*
*leaves*
*3 tablespoons finely chopped*
*fresh oregano leaves*
*3 tablespoons finely chopped*
*fresh flat-leaf (Italian) parsley*
*leaves*

*1 tablespoon finely chopped*
*fresh mint leaves*
*1 tablespoon finely chopped*
*fresh thyme leaves*
*finely grated zest of 1 lemon*
*juice of ½ lemon*
*1 green chilli, cut lengthways,*
*seeded and finely chopped*
*1 red bird's eye chilli, cut*
*lengthways, seeded and*
*finely chopped*
*1 tablespoon smoked paprika*
*175 ml (6 fl oz) light olive oil*

**1/** Combine the vinegars in a bowl with the salt. Stir to dissolve before adding the remaining ingredients and mixing well. Cover and refrigerate for 1 hour before using.

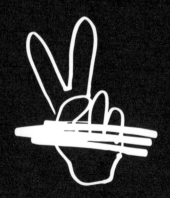

THOUSAND
ISLAND
DRESSING P4

PEAR + WALNUT
CHUTNEY
P8

PICCALILLI P10

CHIMICHURRI
SAUCE      P5

 ← YOGHURT SAUCE **p4**

MANGO CHUTNEY **p8**

CARAMEL CREAM **p24**

HARISSA **p2**

# Mango chutney.

<u>Makes</u> 1 kg (2 lb 3 oz)

1 kg (2 lb 3 oz) firm mango
    flesh, cut into 1 cm (½ in)
    dice
50 g (1¾ oz) fresh ginger,
    peeled and cut into 4 mm
    (¼ in) strips
1 bird's eye chilli, chopped
    (seeds included)
1 red chilli, sliced lengthways,
    seeded and chopped
250 ml (8½ fl oz/1 cup) cider
    vinegar
200 g (7 oz) caster (superfine)
    sugar

1/ Combine all the ingredients in a heavy-based saucepan over medium heat. Bring to the boil, stirring gently, then reduce the heat to low and simmer for 25 minutes. Remove from the heat and cool. This will keep in the refrigerator, packed tightly in sterilised jars, for up to 6 months.

# Pear ± walnut chutney.

<u>Makes</u> 1.25 kg (2 lb 12 oz)

180 g (6½ oz) sultanas
    (golden raisins)
finely grated zest and juice of
    2 oranges
1.2 kg (2 lb 10 oz) firm pear
    flesh, cut into 2 cm (¾ in)
    cubes
220 g (8 oz) tart apple flesh,
    cut into 2 cm (¾ in) cubes
220 g (8 oz) brown onions, diced
450 ml (15 fl oz) apple-cider
    vinegar
400 g (14 oz) jam-setting sugar
150 g (5½ oz) walnuts, toasted
    and chopped
1 teaspoon salt flakes

1/ Put the sultanas in a bowl, pour over the orange zest and juice and leave to stand.

2/ Put the pear, apple and onion in a large heavy-based saucepan or preserving pan over medium heat. Add the vinegar and slowly bring to the boil. Reduce the heat to low and simmer for 30 minutes, until the fruit and onion are tender. Add the sultana mixture and sugar to the pan, raise the heat to high and bring to a simmer. Reduce the heat to low and cook for a further 30 minutes, stirring occasionally throughout, and frequently near the end of cooking, to ensure the contents do not stick and burn. The chutney should be thick with no excess liquid. Remove from the heat and stir in the walnuts and salt. Set aside to cool.

3/ Place the chutney in sterilised jars. The jars of chutney will keep for up to 6 months.

# Romesco sauce.

<u>Makes</u> 600 g (1 lb 5 oz)

1 tablespoon light olive oil
1 garlic bulb, top trimmed off
1 large red capsicum
    (bell pepper)
50 g (1¾ oz/⅓ cup) blanched
    almonds, toasted
200 g (7 oz) tinned whole
    tomatoes
2 tablespoons Arbequina
    olive oil (see page 159)
½ teaspoon salt flakes
1 tablespoon sherry vinegar
1 teaspoon smoked paprika

1/ Preheat the oven to 180°C (350°F).

2/ Rub the light olive oil onto the cut piece of the garlic bulb then wrap the bulb tightly in foil. Roast the garlic in the oven for 1 hour. Remove from the oven and set aside in the foil.

3/ Use a blowtorch, or the open flame of a gas stove burner, to burn and blister the entire surface of the red capsicum. Place it in a bowl and cover tightly with plastic wrap for a few minutes to sweat. Remove the plastic wrap and rub the charred skin away with your fingertips. Use some water to wash away all the black bits and then cut the capsicum in half, discard the seeds and roughly chop the flesh.

4/ Squeeze the garlic flesh from the bulb into a blender or food processor. Add the almonds and blitz for 1 minute. Add the remaining ingredients and process on low speed until you have a coarse-textured sauce. Reserve in the refrigerator until needed. It will last for up to 1 week.

# Dill pickles.

<u>Makes</u> 1.2 kg (2 lb 10 oz)

750 g (1 lb 11 oz) small pickling
    cucumbers
500 ml (17 fl oz/2 cups) white-
    wine vinegar
100 g (3½ oz) golden caster
    (superfine) sugar
1 tablespoon mustard seeds
1 tablespoon salt flakes
1 tablespoon whole black
    peppercorns
½ bunch fresh dill

1/ Top and tail the cucumbers and cut them into quarters lengthways. Pack the cucumber quarters into one large warm sterilised jar or several smaller jars.

2/ Put the vinegar, sugar, mustard seeds, salt and peppercorns in a saucepan over medium–low heat and bring gently to a simmer. Stir to dissolve the sugar then remove the pan from the heat. Set this pickling liquid aside to cool.

3/ Add dill fronds as desired to the jar, or jars, then top with the cooled pickling liquid. Gently tap the jar to remove any air bubbles and top up with more liquid if necessary. Seal tightly and store in the refrigerator. The pickles will be ready to eat in 1 week and will keep for up to 6 months. Keep refrigerated once opened.

# Piccalilli.

**Makes** 2 kg (4 lb 6 oz)

1 cauliflower, cut into small
    florets
1 broccoli head, cut into small
    florets
3 brown onions, peeled and cut
    into 1 cm (½ in) dice
1 bunch spring onions
    (scallions), white part only,
    sliced 5 mm (¼ in) thick
1 cucumber, peeled, seeded
    and cut into 1 cm (½ in) dice
2 large red chillies, chopped
    (seeds included)
1 large green chilli, chopped
    (seeds included)
1 red capsicum (bell pepper),
    cut into 1 cm (½ in) dice
50 g (1¾ oz) salt flakes
350 g (12½ oz) caster
    (superfine) sugar
50 g (1¾ oz) English mustard
    powder
25 g (1 oz) ground turmeric
40 g (1½ oz/⅓ cup) cornflour
    (cornstarch)
600 ml (20½ fl oz) white-wine
    vinegar
300 ml (10½ fl oz) malt vinegar
freshly ground black pepper

**1/** Place all the vegetables in a large bowl and sprinkle over the salt. Mix well and leave to stand for a couple of hours. Rinse the vegetables in cold water and drain them in a colander. Pour the vegetables into a large clean bowl.

**2/** Mix the sugar with the mustard, turmeric and cornflour in a large bowl.

**3/** Bring the vinegars to the boil in a large saucepan then pour one-third of this mixture into the bowl with the dry ingredients. Mix well to form a paste and then return this to the pan with the remaining vinegar and whisk it all together. Reduce the heat to low and cook the thick yellow paste for 3 minutes, stirring slowly and constantly with a heat-resistant spatula.

**4/** Pour the hot mixture into the bowl with the vegetables and mix well. Transfer the mixture to sterilised jars or plastic containers and store in the refrigerator for a day before consuming. This will last up to 6 months, unopened, and for 1 month after opening.

# Pickled mustard seeds.

Makes 500 g (1 lb 2 oz)

*100 g (3½ oz) yellow mustard
    seeds*
*50 g (1¾ oz) caster (superfine)
    sugar*
*2 teaspoons salt flakes*
*150 ml (5 fl oz) chardonnay
    vinegar*

**1/** Place the mustard seeds in a small saucepan and cover with cold water. Bring to the boil then remove from the heat. Drain the seeds and discard the water. Refresh the seeds in cold water and return them to the saucepan. Repeat the previous step three times and reserve the blanched seeds in a bowl or jug.

**2/** Heat 75 ml (2½ fl oz) water and the sugar in a saucepan over medium–low heat and stir until dissolved. Remove from the heat, add the salt and stir until it has dissolved. Stir in the vinegar then strain this pickling liquid over the seeds. Place in the refrigerator, covered, for a minimum of 1 hour. The seeds will last for 2 months.

# Pickled carrot.

Makes 600 g (1 lb 5 oz)

*375 ml (12½ fl oz/1½ cups) rice
    wine vinegar*
*170 g (6 oz/¾ cup) caster
    (superfine) sugar*
*1 teaspoon mustard seeds*
*2 carrots, peeled and
    cut into strips using a
    vegetable peeler*

**1/** Combine the vinegar, sugar and mustard seeds in a small saucepan and bring to the boil. Stir the liquid to dissolve the sugar then remove the pan from the heat. Leave to cool then dress the carrot with a quarter of the liquid.

**2/** Seal or cover and leave to pickle in the refrigerator for a minimum of 3 hours. The rest of the pickling liquid can be stored in the refrigerator for a few weeks and used as needed for quick pickling.

# Pickled daikon.

Makes 600 g (1 lb 5 oz)

*375 ml (12½ fl oz/1½ cups) rice
    wine vinegar*
*170 g (6 oz/¾ cup) caster
    (superfine) sugar*
*1 teaspoon mustard seeds*
*½ daikon (white radish), peeled
    and cut into strips using a
    vegetable peeler*

**1/** Combine the vinegar, sugar and mustard seeds in a small saucepan and bring to the boil. Stir the liquid to dissolve the sugar then remove the pan from the heat. Leave to cool then dress the daikon with a quarter of the liquid.

**2/** Seal or cover and leave to pickle in the refrigerator for a minimum of 3 hours. The rest of the pickling liquid can be stored in the refrigerator for a few weeks and used as needed for quick pickling.

# Sauerkraut.

<u>Makes</u> 750 g (1 lb 11 oz)

*½ savoy cabbage (about
750 g/1 lb 11 oz), thinly
sliced using a mandoline
or sharp knife
10 g (¼ oz) salt flakes
2 teaspoons caraway seeds*

**1/** Place all the ingredients in a large glass bowl. Using clean hands, toss and massage the cabbage to evenly distribute the salt. This will also start to break down the enzymes and release water. Continue to mix the cabbage for 5 minutes, then cover the bowl and leave to stand for 20 minutes at room temperature.

**2/** Pack the cabbage into a sterilised 1 litre (34 fl oz/4 cup) capacity glass jar. Pack the vegetables firmly into the jar using clean hands or a spoon. There should be enough naturally extracted liquid to cover the cabbage but, if not, just top up the jar with boiled and cooled water.

**3/** Weigh the cabbage down with a clean ceramic or stone weight and leave, uncovered, at room temperature. Seal with a lid as soon as fermentation starts – this could be straight away or after a couple of days. You can tell it's ready for the lid when the cabbage stays submerged after the weight is removed.

**4/** Set the jar aside in a cool dark place to ferment, The sauerkraut will be ready after 1 week and will keep for up to 6 months. Once ready, store in the refrigerator and use as required.

# Caramelised onions.

<u>Makes</u> 250 g (9 oz)

*3 red onions, peeled and sliced
salt flakes
1 bird's eye chilli, chopped
80 ml (2½ fl oz/⅓ cup) light
olive oil*

**1/** Place the onions in a 3 litre (101 fl oz/12 cup) capacity, square microwave-safe glass dish with a steam escape lid. Season the onions with salt and stir in the chilli and olive oil. Place the lid on the dish with the steam escape open and place the dish in the microwave. Cook on High (100%) for 10 minutes.

**2/** Remove the dish from the microwave and carefully remove the lid, allowing the steam to escape. Use a fork to mix the wet onions, ensuring everything is well combined. Replace the lid and cook for a further 4 minutes.

**3/** Remove the dish from the microwave and again mix the onions with a fork. Replace the lid and cook for a further 4 minutes. Repeat these steps until the onions start to become thick and jammy. The onions should be dark in colour and the moisture will have evaporated sufficiently for them to be sticky. Store the onions in a container in the refrigerator for up to 4 days.

# Kimchi.

Makes 1 kg (2 lb 3 oz)

800 g (1 lb 12 oz) Chinese
   cabbage (wombok), outer
   leaves discarded
100 g (3½ oz/¾ cup) salt flakes
1 carrot, coarsely grated
3 garlic cloves, finely grated
1 bunch spring onions
   (scallions), white part only,
   thinly sliced
60 g (2 oz) fresh ginger, peeled
   and grated
1 tablespoon caster (superfine)
   sugar
2 tablespoons salt flakes
1 tablespoon fish sauce
2 tablespoons Korean
   fermented chilli paste
   (gochujang) (see page 159)

1/ Slice the cabbage leaves into thick chunks and place them in a bowl. Add the salt and massage the leaves with clean hands for a few minutes. Pour over 600 ml (20½ fl oz) water and again mix with your hands. Cover the bowl and leave to stand for a couple of hours at room temperature.

2/ Drain the water and rinse the cabbage leaves in cold water for a couple of minutes.

3/ In a bowl, mix together the remaining ingredients then add this mixture to the cabbage. Mix well then push into a warm, sterilised jar or ceramic container with an airtight lid. Leave to stand at room temperature overnight before storing in the refrigerator with the lid closed.

4/ Every day for 1 week, remove the kimchi from the refrigerator, open the lid for 5 minutes to let the kimchi breathe, then close the lid and return to the refrigerator. The kimchi will be ready to use after 1 week and will last for a couple of months. Store in the refrigerator and chop it into smaller pieces when serving, if necessary.

# Coleslaw.

Makes 750 g (1 lb 11 oz)

¼ savoy cabbage, shredded
   thinly with a mandoline or
   sharp knife
¼ red onion, thinly sliced
2 carrots, peeled and julienned
juice of ½ lemon
1 teaspoon salt flakes
60 ml (2 fl oz/¼ cup) light
   olive oil

1/ Combine the vegetables in a bowl. Whisk the lemon juice, salt and oil together and dress the vegetables at the moment of serving.

# Roasted tomatoes.

<u>Makes</u> approximately 250 g (9 oz)

*truss of mini tomatoes on the
    vine (about 12–16 tomatoes)*
*drizzle of light olive oil*
*salt flakes*
*freshly ground black pepper*

**1/** Preheat the oven to 140°C (275°F). Line a baking tray with baking paper.

**2/** Place the tomato vine on the baking tray, drizzle with olive oil and season with salt and pepper. Cook the tomatoes in the oven for 30 minutes. Remove from the oven and allow to cool. Use the tomatoes as required by squashing them into sandwiches.

# Tunisian carrot salad.

<u>Makes</u> 1 kg (2 lb 3 oz)

*1 kg (2 lb 3 oz) carrots*
*75 ml (2½ fl oz) light olive oil*
*100 ml (3½ fl oz) Harissa
    vinaigrette (page 3)*
*50 g (1¾ oz) kalamata olives,
    cheeks only*
*10 g (¼ oz/⅓ cup) fresh flat-
    leaf (Italian) parsley leaves,
    chopped*
*10 g (¼ oz/⅓ cup) fresh
    coriander (cilantro) leaves,
    chopped*

**1/** Preheat the oven to 140°C (275°F).

**2/** Peel the carrots, cut them into 5 × 1 cm (2 × ½ in) batons and roll them in the olive oil. Season with salt and pepper. Place the carrots, evenly spaced apart, in a roasting tin. Cover tightly with aluminium foil and cook for 30–45 minutes until very tender. Leaving the foil in place, allow the carrots to cool at room temperature.

**3/** Gently toss the carrots in the vinaigrette with the olives and herbs and serve.

# Fried eggs.

<u>Makes</u> 4

4 eggs
100 ml (3½ fl oz) light olive oil
50 g (1¾ oz) unsalted butter
salt flakes
freshly ground black pepper

**1/** Carefully crack the eggs into four separate bowls to ensure they are all good, intact and free of shell.

**2/** Place the oil and butter in a large non-stick frying pan over the lowest heat. Slowly pour each egg into the pan and gently cook the eggs. While cooking, carefully lift each egg with a spatula to ensure it doesn't stick to the bottom of the pan. Cook the eggs until the whites are fully cooked and the yolks are set and runny. Sprinkle salt and pepper over each egg and serve immediately.

# Cheesy omelette square.

<u>Makes</u> 1 omelette

2 eggs
salt flakes
freshly ground black pepper
20 g (¾ oz) unsalted butter
1 slice cheddar, cut from a block
    approximately 8 cm (3¼ in)
    square and 3 mm (⅛ in) thick

**1/** Lightly beat the eggs and season with salt and pepper.

**2/** Heat an 18 cm (7 in) non-stick frying pan over medium heat. Add the butter and let it melt. Cook just until the butter starts to froth then pour in the egg. Cook for 1 minute until the omelette has set on the bottom of the pan. Add the cheese slice to the centre of the omelette and use a small palette knife to fold the omelette flaps inwards to cover the cheese. Remove the pan from the heat and use a spatula to transfer the omelette onto your sandwich or plate.

# Potato chips.

<u>Makes</u> 400 g (14 oz)

6 bintje (yellow finn), maris piper
    or other good frying potatoes,
    washed but not peeled
1 litre (34 fl oz/4 cups) canola
    or sunflower oil for frying
salt flakes

**1/** Thinly slice the potatoes and place them in a large colander. Rinse the potatoes in cold water until the water runs clear. Drain the potatoes and dry them on paper towel.

**2/** Heat the oil in a saucepan to 180°C (350°F), using a thermometer to check the temperature. Cook small batches of potatoes, stirring regularly, until golden and crispy, about 3 minutes. Remove the potatoes from the pan using a slotted spoon and drain them on paper towel. Season the potato chips with the salt and serve.

KIMCHI *p13*

CARAMELISED ONIONS *p12*

ROASTED
TOMATOES *p14*

DILL PICKLES *p9*

SAUERKRAUT *p12*

VANILLA CHERRIES *p24*

TUNISIAN CARROT SALAD *p14*

PICKLED MUSTARD SEEDS *p11*

# Pita bread.

canola oil spray
light olive oil or garlic-infused
    olive oil
salt flakes

Dough
450 g (1 lb) unbleached plain
    (all-purpose) flour
½ teaspoon salt flakes
¼ teaspoon caster (superfine)
    sugar
½ teaspoon dried yeast
60 ml (2 fl oz/¼ cup) olive oil
275 ml (9½ fl oz) warm water

1/ Put all the dough ingredients in the bowl of a freestanding electric mixer fitted with the dough hook. Mix on low speed for approximately 10 minutes, or knead by hand until the dough is smooth and elastic.

2/ Roll the dough into golfball-sized balls, dust with flour and place on a baking tray. Spray lightly with canola oil and cover gently with plastic wrap. Leave to prove in a warm place for approximately 30 minutes to 1 hour. When the dough is ready it should have increased in size and an indentation will be left when you touch it.

3/ On a lightly floured work surface, roll out each ball of dough into an 18–20 cm (7–8 in) circle. Brush the circles with olive oil or garlic-infused olive oil, then chargrill on a hot barbecue or in a flat non-stick frying pan over high heat. After less than a minute the bread should puff up nicely. Turn it over and cook the other side.

4/ Brush the cooked bread with more olive oil and sprinkle with salt. Stack the cooked breads on top of each other and cover with a tea towel (dish towel) to stop them drying out.

# Maple-cured bacon.

Makes 12 slices

12 thin rashers (slices) cold-
    smoked bacon, about 10 cm
    (4 in) in length
100 g (3½ oz) raw (demerara)
    sugar
100 ml (3½ fl oz) good-quality
    maple syrup

1/ Take one rasher of bacon and sprinkle a pinch of raw sugar on top, then drizzle over a few drops of maple syrup. Place another rasher of bacon on top of the previous slice and repeat with the raw sugar and maple syrup. Continue until all of the rashers are used. Store tightly in a zip-lock bag in the refrigerator for 12 hours.

2/ Preheat the oven to 170°C (340°F).

3/ Remove the bacon from the bag, separate the rashers and place them on a baking tray lined with baking paper. Lay another sheet of baking paper on top of the bacon and rest another baking tray of the same size on top. This will ensure the bacon stays flat during cooking. Bake for 10–12 minutes or until the bacon is cooked and crisp. Leave to cool then remove the top tray.

# Chicken liver parfait.

**Makes** 1 kg (2 lb 3 oz)

*600 g (1 lb 5 oz) chicken livers,*
  *cleaned and sinew cut away*
*3 eggs*
*2 egg yolks*
*125 ml (4 fl oz/½ cup)*
  *Reduction (see below),*
  *cooled*
*400 g (14 oz) unsalted butter,*
  *melted*
*salt flakes*
*white pepper*

*Reduction*
*175 ml (6 fl oz) Madeira*
*175 ml (6 fl oz) port*
*3 French shallots, peeled and*
  *sliced*
*1 garlic clove, peeled and sliced*
*1 tablespoon chopped fresh*
  *thyme leaves*
*1 bay leaf*
*1 tablespoon freshly ground*
  *black pepper*
*100 ml (3½ fl oz) lamb stock*

**1/** For the reduction, combine the Madeira, port, shallots, garlic, thyme, bay leaf and pepper in a heavy-based saucepan over medium–high heat. Bring to the boil and cook until the mixture has reduced by half, about 6–10 minutes. Add the lamb stock and reduce by half again, about 3–5 minutes. Remove the pan from the heat and allow the reduction to cool before straining and reserving until needed.

**2/** For the parfait, process the chicken livers in a food processor or blender on high speed until you have a very fine purée. Pass the mixture through a fine sieve.

**3/** Clean the blender jug then transfer the purée back to the blender and blitz on medium speed. Add the eggs and egg yolks, one at a time, then the reduction, followed by the butter. Season the mixture and pour it into five small 200 ml (7 fl oz) ramekins.

**4/** Preheat the oven to 120°C (250°F).

**5/** Place the ramekins in a baking tin and add hot water to come halfway up the sides of the ramekins. Tightly fix aluminium foil over the top of the tin and place it in the oven. Cook for 1 hour until the parfaits have set and the core temperature of the parfaits is higher than 65°C (150°F). Remove the tin from the oven and allow to cool before removing the foil and storing the parfaits, covered, in the refrigerator. These can be frozen, covered. If frozen, place them in the refrigerator the night before, and thaw thoroughly before use.

# Barbecued soy caramel pork belly.

*800 g (1 lb 12 oz) pork belly,
  sliced 1 cm (½ in) thick*

*<u>Soy caramel</u>
100 g (3½ oz) caster (superfine)
  sugar
80 ml (2½ fl oz/⅓ cup) soy
  sauce
1 tablespoon fish sauce
1 tablespoon lime juice
1 tablespoon finely chopped
  fresh coriander (cilantro)
  stalks
1 tablespoon finely grated
  fresh ginger
1 bird's eye chilli, seeded and
  chopped
1 garlic clove, finely grated*

**1/** For the soy caramel, combine the sugar and 60 ml (2 fl oz/¼ cup) water in a small saucepan over medium heat. Bring to the boil and cook the syrup until it is a deep golden-amber colour.

**2/** Remove the pan from the heat and stir in the soy sauce, fish sauce and lime juice. Add the coriander, ginger, chilli and garlic and leave to cool.

**3/** Lay the pork slices in a glass dish and pour over the soy caramel. Turn the slices of pork over in the dish to ensure the caramel has covered them all. Cover and leave in the refrigerator overnight.

**4/** Remove the pork slices from the dish and place them on a tray. Drain the soy caramel, pour it into a saucepan over medium heat and bring it to the boil. Remove the pan from the heat and strain the caramel through a fine sieve and reserve.

**5/** Heat a barbecue to high and cook each slice of pork for around 3 minutes on each side.


# Marinated pork belly.

*5 tablespoons Korean fermented
  chilli paste (gochujang) (see
  page 159)
4 garlic cloves, finely grated
3 tablespoons caster (superfine)
  sugar
30 g (1 oz) fresh ginger, peeled
  and finely grated
2 spring onions (scallions),
  white part only, thinly sliced
1 tablespoon freshly ground
  black pepper
60 ml (2 fl oz/¼ cup) toasted
  sesame oil
12 fresh, thick slices pork belly*

**1/** Combine all the ingredients, except the pork, in a bowl and mix well. Add the pork slices and mix to cover completely in the marinade. Leave, covered, in the refrigerator for 1 hour.

**2/** Preheat the oven to 180°C (350°F).

**3/** Remove the pork from the refrigerator. Arrange the slices of pork, evenly spaced apart, on a non-stick baking tray. Cook for 25 minutes, turning the pork once during cooking.

# Roasted marinated pork shoulder.

**<u>Makes</u> 16 slices**

2 kg (4 lb 6 oz) pork shoulder,
    upper half (also known as
    Boston butt – you need to
    pre-order this from your
    butcher)
500 g (1 lb 2 oz) pineapple
    flesh, cut into chunks
    then blended to a coarse
    consistency
2 tablespoons finely chopped
    fresh oregano leaves
3 tablespoons cumin seeds,
    lightly toasted
4 garlic cloves, finely grated
3 large green chillies, cut
    lengthways, seeded
    and chopped
2 jalapeños, cut lengthways,
    seeded and chopped
juice and finely grated zest
    of 2 limes
40 g (1½ oz) fresh ginger,
    peeled and finely grated
80 ml (2½ fl oz/⅓ cup) light
    olive oil

**1/** Remove the excess fat from the pork and use a sharp knife to score diagonal cuts in the top of the meat.

**2/** Combine the remaining ingredients in a bowl then rub the mixture all over the pork.

**3/** Transfer everything to a glass bowl and again massage the meat well with the marinade. Cover with plastic wrap and leave in the refrigerator overnight.

**4/** The next day remove the pork from the refrigerator and preheat the oven to 150°C (300°F).

**5/** Drain the marinade from the pork and place the meat in a roasting tin. Cook the pork in the oven for 1 hour. Remove the tin from the oven and cover with foil. Reduce the oven temperature to 110°C (230°F) and cook for a further 7 hours, or until the meat is super tender. Slice as needed and, if desired, barbecue each slice to obtain char marks before using in melts or sandwiches.

# Cath's slow-roasted lamb shoulder.

<u>**Makes**</u> **1.5 kg (3 lb 5 oz)**

*finely grated zest and juice
    of 2 lemons*
*2 teaspoons dijon mustard*
*200 ml (7 fl oz) light olive oil*
*2 teaspoons dried oregano*
*2 tablespoons chopped fresh
    thyme leaves*
*2 tablespoons chopped fresh
    rosemary leaves*
*5 garlic cloves, finely grated*
*1.5 kg (3 lb 5 oz) lamb shoulder,
    boned and excess fat
    removed (not all)*
*salt flakes*
*freshly ground black pepper*

**1/** Combine all the ingredients in a large bowl, except the lamb, salt and pepper. Add the lamb and turn to coat it thoroughly with the marinade. Refrigerate for a minimum of 12 hours and up to 24.

**2/** Preheat the oven to 150°C (300°F).

**3/** Place the meat in a roasting tin and season well with salt and pepper. Roast the lamb for 3–5 hours, basting it regularly with the cooking juices and fat. When the meat is tender and cooked, leave it to rest before pulling it apart using a fork and tongs.

(T⬛⬛⬛⬛⬛⬛⬛EED)

# Vanilla custard.

<u>Makes</u> 700 g (1 lb 9 oz)

275 ml (9½ fl oz) thickened
    (whipping) cream
275 ml (9½ fl oz) full-cream
    (whole) milk
1 vanilla bean, seeds scraped
95 g (3¼ oz) caster (superfine)
    sugar
20 g (¾ oz) cornflour
    (cornstarch)
3 egg yolks

1/ Combine the cream, milk, vanilla seeds and pod in a saucepan over medium–low heat. Bring to a simmer, then remove the pan from the heat and discard the vanilla pod.

2/ Put the sugar, cornflour and egg yolks in a bowl and whisk well until the mixture pales and thickens.

3/ Pour one-third of the hot milk and cream mixture onto the egg and sugar mixture and whisk well to combine. Pour this mixture back into the saucepan with the remaining milk and cream and mix well with a spatula or wooden spoon.

4/ Place the pan back over medium–low heat and whisk constantly while cooking the custard, until it starts to boil and bubble, about 1 minute. Cook at this temperature for a further 20 seconds, stirring constantly.

5/ Serve immediately. Alternatively, transfer the custard to the bowl of a freestanding electric mixer fitted with the paddle attachment. Mix the custard on a low to medium speed until it cools to room temperature. This will keep it smooth. Store the custard in the refrigerator until needed.

# White chocolate cream.

<u>Makes</u> 360 g (12½ oz)

120 g (4½ oz) white chocolate,
    melted
240 ml (8 fl oz) thickened
    (whipping) cream

1/ Put the melted chocolate in a bowl.

2/ Put 80 ml (2½ fl oz/⅓ cup) of the cream in a saucepan over medium heat and bring to the boil, then pour the cream over the melted chocolate. Leave for 30 seconds before stirring the cream and chocolate together well using a spatula.

3/ Stir in the remaining cold cream. Transfer the mixture to a covered container and place in the refrigerator for a minimum of 1 hour before using.

4/ Whip the white chocolate cream to thick ribbon stage with an electric mixer or hand whisk before using.

# Caramel cream.

**Makes** 750 g (1 lb 11 oz)

*185 ml (6 fl oz/¾ cup) thickened
(whipping) cream
225 g (8 oz) caster (superfine)
sugar
4 eggs
4 g (¼ oz) gold-strength
gelatine leaves, soaked in
water and excess water
squeezed out
165 g (6 oz) unsalted butter,
softened*

**1/** Place the cream in a saucepan over medium heat and bring to the boil. Immediately remove the pan from the heat and set aside.

**2/** Place a larger saucepan over medium heat for a minute to get hot, then gradually add the sugar to the pan in three batches. After adding each batch, stir the sugar with a wooden spoon or heat-resistant spatula to dissolve and cook it to a deep amber colour. Once all the sugar is in and you have a golden caramel, add half the scalded cream. Take care as this mixture will expand furiously and the steam is extremely hot. Whisk the mixture and add the remaining cream until everything is combined.

**3/** Whisk the eggs by hand in a bowl then pour over one-third of the caramel mixture. Continue to mix well for 30 seconds, then pour this mixture back into the saucepan. Reduce the heat to low and cook until the mixture reaches 82°C (180°F), using a digital thermometer to check the temperature. Stir constantly at this stage.

**4/** Remove the pan from the stove and whisk in the soaked and drained gelatine and the butter until you have a smooth cream. Pour the cream into a container and refrigerate for a minimum of 4 hours before using.

# Vanilla cherries.

**Makes** 750 g (1 lb 11 oz)

*500 g (1 lb 2 oz) frozen pitted
black cherries
150 g (5½ oz) jam-setting sugar
1 vanilla bean, seeds scraped
finely grated zest of ½ lemon*

**1/** Defrost the frozen cherries overnight in the refrigerator in a sieve or colander set over a container to catch any juices.

**2/** The next day, put the cherry juice, 100 ml (3½ fl oz) water, the sugar, vanilla seeds and lemon zest in a saucepan over medium–low heat and gently bring to the boil. Add the cherries and again bring to the boil before removing the pan from the heat and chilling in the refrigerator overnight before using.

# Candied orange slices.

**Makes** 750 g (1 lb 11 oz)

3 oranges, cut in half, with skin
    on, and sliced 5 mm (¼ in)
    thick
375 g (13 oz) caster (superfine)
    sugar

**1/** Place the orange slices in a saucepan and cover with cold
water. Simmer for about 1–1½ hours until the pith and skin are
translucent. Discard the cooking liquid.

**2/** Put the sugar and 250 ml (8½ fl oz/1 cup) water in a saucepan
over medium heat and bring to the boil. Reduce the heat, add the
orange slices and simmer for 30 minutes until the orange is tender
and the syrup has reduced. Leave to cool in the syrup and store
in the refrigerator.

# Nut crumble mix.

**Makes** 245 g (8½ oz)

35 g (1¼ oz/⅓ cup) ground
    almonds
60 g (2 oz) plain (all-purpose)
    flour
45 g (1½ oz) light muscovado
    sugar (see page 159)
45 g (1½ oz) unsalted butter,
    melted and cooled
20 g (¾ oz) hazelnuts, shelled
    and chopped
20 g (¾ oz) blanched almonds,
    chopped
20 g (¾ oz) walnuts, chopped

**1/** Put the ground almonds, flour, muscovado sugar, melted butter
and nuts in a bowl and mix with your fingertips to form a nut
crumble. You can use the mixture raw or cooked.

# Press.

(SQUASHED THINGS)

# Toasted Reuben: emmental, pastrami, sauerkraut, thousand island dressing, dill pickles ± potato chips.

Close your eyes and you could be in New York – actually, this is better. I love the classic combination of Swiss cheese, pastrami and pickles. The pastrami used here is so good. I get mine expertly sliced by master butcher Gary McBean from Gary's Meats at Prahran Market in Melbourne, and it's just sensational. Speak to your local butcher about yours.

## Pro tips
If you take the time to make as many of these sandwich fillings as you can, then you will be rewarded. The thousand island dressing is a fantastic addition and worth spending the time on as it's miles better than anything you can buy in a store.

## Makes
4

## Prep time
13 minutes

## Toasting method
Toasted sandwich press

## Bread
8 slices light or dark rye sourdough loaf

90 g (3 oz) unsalted butter
20 Cape Grim brisket pastrami slices
8 slices emmental
8 Dill pickles (page 9)
6 heaped tablespoons Sauerkraut (page 12), drained
4 heaped tablespoons Thousand island dressing (page 4)
Potato chips (page 15), to serve

**1/** Build the sandwiches, butter side down, on four squares of baking paper for ease of movement. Butter four slices of rye bread and turn them over.

**2/** Liberally spread butter on the inside of the rye slices then place the pastrami on top. Add the slices of cheese and a few dill pickles before adding a heaped tablespoon of drained sauerkraut to each slice. Finish with a large tablespoon of thousand island dressing on each slice. Butter both sides of the remaining rye slices and top the sandwiches off. Gently press down.

**3/** Heat a toasted sandwich press and cook the sandwiches until the cheese is just starting to melt. Cut the sandwiches in half and serve with potato chips.

# Ploughman's: smoked leg ham, cheddar ± chutney.

One of my favourite jokes from the legendary British comedian Tommy Cooper was: Two cannibals were eating a clown and one said to the other, 'Does this taste funny to you?' Quality! Another one that tickled me was, 'I ate a ploughman's lunch today (pause)…he was livid'. Not quite as funny written down, but YouTube him – he was hilarious. Anyway…

### Pro tips
A ploughman's is one of life's great ambiguous dishes. Anything is allowed on a ploughman's, so choose your meat and cheese to taste. Any great cloth-bound cheddar will do fine. I have used a soy and linseed sourdough from Michael James, the baker at my local, Tivoli Road Bakery, but you can use whatever you fancy.

### Makes
4

### Prep time
13 minutes

### Toasting method
Toasted sandwich press

### Bread
8 slices soy and linseed sourdough loaf

4 tablespoons Pear + walnut chutney (page 8)
8 thick slices smoked leg ham
salt flakes
freshly ground black pepper
200 g (7 oz) Montgomery cheddar, grated
100 g (3½ oz) Monterey Jack, grated
Piccalilli (page 10), to serve
sorrel leaves (see page 159), to serve
Sweet mustard dressing (page 3), to dress the sorrel
Dill pickles (page 9), to serve
extra cheese and ham, to serve

**1/** Build the sandwiches, butter side down, on four squares of baking paper for ease of movement. Butter four slices of bread and turn them over.

**2/** Evenly spread the pear and walnut chutney on the bread. Arrange the ham on each slice and season with salt and pepper before adding the grated cheeses. Butter both sides of the remaining slices and top the sandwiches off.

**3/** Heat a toasted sandwich press and cook the sandwiches until they are golden brown and crispy on the outside and the cheese has melted. Remove from the press and serve with piccalilli, sorrel leaves dressed with the sweet mustard dressing, pickles and more cheese and ham on the side.

# Gorgonzola, pumpkin, maple-cured bacon ± caramelised onion w̲ maple syrup.

There's a lot going on here flavour-wise, but everything works together well as a team. Shop around for the best-quality maple syrup you can find. You'll be amazed at the difference between a cheaper fake syrup and a real Canadian variety.

## Pro tips
The piccante-style gorgonzola is perfect for melting in this sandwich, and here it's mixed with another milder, good melting cheese so it's not too strong. I've gone for a light rye sourdough again to give a crunch to the sandwich, and it's robust enough to hold all the filling in one place. You can cure your own bacon in maple (page 18) or you can buy it from a good butcher.

## Makes
4

## Prep time
25–30 minutes

## Toasting method
Toasted sandwich press and oven

## Bread
8 slices light rye sourdough loaf

500 g (1 lb 2 oz) Jap pumpkin (squash), peeled and seeds removed
60 ml (2 fl oz/¼ cup) light olive oil
salt flakes
freshly ground black pepper
100 g (3½ oz) gorgonzola piccante (Mauri), crumbled or grated
200 g (7 oz) Monterey Jack, grated
80 g (2¾ oz) Caramelised onions (page 12)
12 rashers (slices) Maple-cured bacon (page 18), cooked
100 g (3½ oz) unsalted butter, softened
drizzle of good-quality maple syrup

**1/** Preheat the oven to 150°C (300°F).

**2/** Slice the pumpkin into 2 cm (¾ in) thick pieces – in total you will need around eight pieces of pumpkin of a similar size. Toss them in a bowl with the oil, salt and pepper. Place the pumpkin pieces on a non-stick, lipped baking tray and cover tightly with foil to seal. Place the tray in the oven and cook the pumpkin for 15–20 minutes until it is just cooked. Remove the tray from the oven, remove the foil and set the pumpkin aside to cool. It should be just soft to the touch, but not overcooked.

**3/** To assemble the sandwiches, mix the two cheeses together in a bowl. Lay out four slices of bread and place the pumpkin slices on top followed by a scattering of caramelised onions and then three rashers of bacon. Add the cheese mixture evenly on top of the bacon and close the sandwich with the remaining slices of bread.

**4/** Lightly spread butter on the surface of the sandwiches, then flip the sandwiches over and butter the bottom. Heat a toasted sandwich press and cook the sandwiches until golden brown and crispy on the outside with a melted cheese interior. Remove, cut in half and serve with a good drizzle of maple syrup.

# Jamón, manchego, tomato ± olive oil toasted baguette.

I have travelled in Spain extensively, both working and holidaying there many times. I absolutely love the place, people, climate and especially the food. Whenever I am in Spain I stuff myself with tomato on bread with olive oil for breakfast, and I usually have a ham, tomato and cheese baguette to keep me going in the afternoon. This is my version of the two combined.

### Pro tips
Use the best-quality jamón you can afford. The real secret and thrill to this sandwich is the big chunks of tomato and the garlic aroma from rubbing the toast with a cut clove. Use the ripest and juiciest tomatoes you can get your hands on.

### Makes
4

### Prep time
12–14 minutes

### Toasting method
Toasted sandwich press

### Bread
4 mini baguettes, sliced lengthways

80 ml (2½ fl oz/⅓ cup) Arbequina olive oil (see page 159)
2 garlic cloves, halved
8 small ripe truss tomatoes, halved
12 thin slices jamón ibérico de bellota (see page 159)
12 slices manchego
salt flakes

**1/** Heat a toasted sandwich press. Drizzle some of the olive oil inside a baguette and place it on the sandwich press to lightly toast the inside. Remove the baguette and gently rub the toasted surface with the cut garlic pieces. Repeat with the remaining three baguettes.

**2/** Use a teaspoon to scoop the seeds and flesh from the ripe tomatoes and spread it on the inside of each baguette. Add four tomato halves per baguette, then three slices of jamón, three slices of manchego and some salt flakes.

**3/** Close the sandwiches and rub some olive oil on the outside of each baguette. Heat a toasted sandwich press and cook the baguettes until crispy on the outside. Remove, cut the baguettes in half and serve.

# Marinated Korean pork belly w̲ kimchi ± fried egg.

**So good – I could eat this every day. The pork is taken to the next level with the funky kimchi. And then there's the egg. Shut up!**

### Pro tip
You can make your own kimchi using the recipe on page 13, but there are some great store-bought kimchis available.

### Makes
4

### Prep time
14 minutes

### Toasting method
Cast-iron sandwich grill pan

### Bread
4 brioche buns, sliced lengthways

8 cos (romaine) lettuce leaves, washed
600 g (1 lb 5 oz) Marinated pork belly slices (page 20)
4 tablespoons chopped Kimchi (page 13)
80 g (2¾ oz) Pickled carrot (page 11)
4 Fried eggs (page 15)

**1/** Place the cast-iron pan and lid together and heat them for 5 minutes on the stove top over medium heat. Lift the lid and add both halves of the brioche buns to the grill. Toast for 1 minute to bar-mark the insides.

**2/** Remove the buns and add lettuce leaves to each. Evenly distribute the cooked pork belly slices, chopped kimchi and pickled carrot. Prepare the eggs, top the sandwiches with an egg on each and serve with the toasted lid on the side.

# Cath's slow-roasted lamb shoulder toasted pita. *THE BOSS!!!*

**My wife, Cath, makes an amazing slow-roasted lamb. We cook a decent-sized one at the weekend and have it as leftovers in various dishes during the next few days. Pulled lamb in this kebab style melt is the way to go, though.**

## Pro tips
The pita breads on page 18 are dead easy to make so give them a try. Marinate the lamb the day before and you are good to go for a slow-cooked Sunday roast.

## Makes
4

## Prep time
12 minutes

## Toasting method
Toasted sandwich press

## Bread
4 pita breads (page 18), or use store-bought pita

*600 g (1 lb 5 oz) Cath's slow-roasted lamb shoulder (page 22), pulled, warm*
*½ red onion, thinly sliced*
*1 handful rocket (arugula)*
*200 g (7 oz) Yoghurt sauce (page 4)*

**1/** Make four toasted pita rolls at once by laying them out on a board. Evenly distribute the lamb pieces and add some red onion, rocket and a big dollop of yoghurt sauce to each. Roll the pita breads up tightly.

**2/** Heat a toasted sandwich press and cook the pita bread rolls until hot and toasted then serve.

# Cubano: barbecued marinated pork shoulder, emmental ± dill pickle.

The 'Cuban' sandwich originated in Florida, probably catering to the tastes of local immigrant workers. There seem to be many variations but essentially this is a ham and cheese melt and this is my version.

## Pro tips

Marinate the meat for the Roasted marinated pork shoulder (page 21) overnight and have the meat in the oven the next day by 10 am at the latest. The meat can then be enjoyed for dinner, and the left-over pieces refrigerated and then used for barbecued Cuban sandwiches the next day. I have used baguettes, but you could use a brioche bun or try to find a real 'Cubano' loaf, which is a soft, oval-shaped baguette.

## Makes
**4**

## Prep time
**20 minutes**

## Toasting method
**Cast-iron sandwich grill pan and oven**

## Bread
**4 Cuban loaves or
4 individual baguettes,
cut in half lengthways**

200 g (7 oz) Mayonnaise
(page 2), or use store-bought
Kewpie mayonnaise
2 garlic cloves, grated
4 tablespoons finely chopped
fresh coriander (cilantro)
leaves
salt flakes
freshly ground black pepper
8 cos (romaine) lettuce leaves
12 slices Roasted marinated
pork shoulder (page 21),
lightly charred on a hot
barbecue
8 Dill pickles (page 9), sliced
lengthways
12 slices emmental or gruyère
American mustard

**1/** Place the cast-iron grill pan and lid together and heat them for 5 minutes on the stove top over medium heat. Lift the lid, open up the baguette and place it on the grill. Toast for 1 minute to bar-mark the inside of the bun, then remove from the heat. Repeat with the remaining baguettes.

**2/** Combine the mayonnaise with the grated garlic, chopped coriander and salt and pepper to taste and spread this liberally on one side of each baguette. Fill the sandwiches first with the lettuce and then the barbecued pork, followed by the pickles and the cheese slices. Finish with as much American mustard as you like and close the sandwiches.

**3/** Preheat the oven to 180°C (350°F). Lift the lid on the cast-iron grill pan and place a baguette inside. Top with the hot lid and press down to squeeze the sandwich shut. Transfer the pan to the oven and cook for 6 minutes to toast and melt the cheese. Remove from the oven. Repeat with the remaining baguettes, then serve.

# Picanha steak, chimichurri, emmental ± egg.

Steak and eggs. It gets no better – except with cheese on top and an amazing chimichurri sauce, all stuffed in a baguette. This will keep you going all day. Picanha is a thin cut of beef popular in Brazil and perfect for a steak sandwich. You need to speak to your local butcher to order specialised cuts of meat. I go to Gary's Quality Meats at Prahran Market in Melbourne.

### Pro tips
The chimichurri is a great marinade and sauce and can be used with so many dishes. For the bread I have used individual baguettes, but you can use whatever you like. However, I would recommend a firmer bread than a softer one, as the sandwich may go soggy with the steak juices, sauce and egg yolk.

### Makes
4

### Prep time
22 minutes

### Toasting method
Cast-iron sandwich grill pan and grill (broiler)

### Bread
4 individual baguettes

60 ml (2 fl oz/¼ cup) light olive oil
8 thin slices picanha steak (sirloin cap), at room temperature
salt flakes
freshly ground black pepper
8 slices emmental, comté or gruyère
4 baby cos (romaine) lettuce leaves
8 Roasted tomatoes (page 14), halved
100 g (3½ oz) Chimichurri sauce (page 5)
4 Fried eggs (page 15)

1/ Heat a cast-iron sandwich grill pan on the stove top over medium heat for 5 minutes. Keep the lid off at this stage.

2/ Brush the oil over the steaks and cook them, four at a time, in the hot pan for 2 minutes. Turn them over and cook for a further minute, then remove them from the heat. Season with salt and pepper and leave the steaks to rest while you cook the remaining four steaks the same way. Leave these to rest for 2 minutes.

3/ Wipe the cast-iron sandwich grill pan with some paper towel and reheat it, with the lid on, over medium heat for another 5 minutes. Lift the lid, open up the baguette and place it on the grill. Toast to bar-mark the inside of the baguette halves for a minute, then remove from the heat. Repeat with the remaining baguettes.

4/ Preheat a grill (broiler). Place the cheese on the toasted insides of the baguettes and melt the cheese under the grill. Cool slightly before adding two lettuce leaves to each baguette. Add four roasted tomato halves and place two cooked picanha steaks on top of the tomatoes. Drizzle a little of the cooking juices over the steaks and spoon over the chimichurri sauce. Add a fried egg to each one, top with the cheesy baguette lids and serve.

# Bacon, tomato, comté, Montgomery cheddar, spring onion ± pickled mustard seeds.

**And on the seventh day God created bacon, and all was good.**

## Pro tip
These mustard seeds are deffo worth a go, and they work well in a million things, such as salads, dressings, accompaniments and, of course, sandwiches.

## Makes
4

## Prep time
13–14 minutes

## Toasting method
Toasted sandwich press

## Bread
8 slices white sandwich loaf

140 g (5 oz) unsalted butter, softened
1 tablespoon hot English mustard (I like Colemans)
12 cold-smoked bacon rashers (slices), cooked
4 small ripe truss tomatoes, thinly sliced
salt flakes
freshly ground black pepper
160 g (5½ oz) comté, grated
100 g (3½ oz) Montgomery cheddar, grated
2 spring onions (scallions), white part only, thinly sliced
60 g (2 oz) Pickled mustard seeds (page 11)

**1/** Butter four slices of bread and scrape a thin layer of English mustard on each slice. Place three rashers of bacon on each. Add the tomato slices on top and season with salt and pepper.

**2/** Combine the grated cheeses in a bowl with the spring onion and evenly distribute this mixture on top of the tomato.

**3/** Spread butter on the remaining slices of bread and spread the pickled mustard seeds on top. Close the sandwich by inverting this slice on top of the cheese and pressing down gently.

**4/** Heat a toasted sandwich press and butter one side of each sandwich. Place the buttered side on the hot grill then butter the top with the remaining butter. Close the press and cook the sandwiches for 5–6 minutes until they are golden brown and crispy with a melted cheese interior.

# Barbecued soy caramel pork belly toasted banh mi.

**OMG – so good. This is normally served in a Vietnamese baguette, but I have opted for a simple brioche bun. This is such an amazing combo. If you are not used to eating these flavours, I urge you to give this a go. It's magic.**

### Pro tips
The pickles add crunch and relief from the sticky pork and rich chicken liver parfait and the soy caramel marinade is a revelation and can be used for so much more than this sandwich. (It's great for a roast pork marinade.)

### Makes
4

### Prep time
16 minutes

### Toasting method
**Toasted sandwich press and grill (broiler)**

### Bread
**4 brioche buns, cut in half lengthways**

80 g (2¾ oz) unsalted butter, softened

80 g (2¾ oz) Chicken liver parfait (page 19)

140 g (5 oz) Asiago Pressato, grated

100 g (3½ oz) Monterey Jack, grated

12 slices Barbecued soy caramel pork belly (page 20), plus 4 tablespoons soy caramel (reserved from the pork)

80 g (2¾ oz) Pickled carrot (page 11)

80 g (2¾ oz) Pickled daikon (page 11)

1 green chilli, seeded and thinly sliced

½ red bird's eye chilli, seeded and thinly sliced

½ cucumber, peeled, seeded and cut into 6 cm (2½ in) batons

4 tablespoons fresh coriander (cilantro) leaves, plus extra to serve if desired

4 tablespoons Mayonnaise (page 2), or use store-bought Kewpie mayonnaise

**1/** Preheat a grill (broiler). Butter the four bottom halves of the brioche buns and spread the chicken liver parfait evenly on top. Distribute and flatten the grated cheeses on the inside of the top part of the bun and drizzle a tablespoon of the soy caramel onto each. Grill (broil) these cheesy top parts of the bun to melt the cheese and toast the bun, then reserve.

**2/** Arrange three slices of cooked pork belly on top of the parfait on each slice and then add the pickled carrot, daikon, sliced green and red chillies and cucumber. Add the coriander and mayonnaise and top with the cheesy bun half.

**3/** Heat a toasted sandwich press and cook the buns for a minute or two to flatten them and press the fillings together. Cut in half and serve with fresh coriander, if desired.

OMG
OMG
OMG

KEWPIE
MAYONNAISE

300 g

キユーピー マヨネーズ

KEWPIE MAYONNAIS

# Roast beef ± Tunisian carrot salad.

**My wife, Cath, has been making the Tunisian carrot salad (page 14) for years and it is sensational. We have it as a side to roast beef and sometimes have leftovers. So I thought, why not put it all together in a melt?**

### Pro tips
Those caramelised onions come in handy again and the carrots are cooked in such a way that they are sweet and tender but not mushy. I have used amazing Turkish bread made by a friend of mine, Michael James, as I think it works really well with the flavours of carrot and harissa.

### Makes
4

### Prep time
13 minutes

### Toasting method
**Toasted sandwich press and grill (broiler)**

### Bread
**four 10 cm (4 in) pieces Turkish bread, cut in half**

*8 slices comté or gruyère*
*320 g (11½ oz) Tunisian carrot salad (page 14)*
*16 Roasted tomatoes (page 14)*
*80 g (2¾ oz) Caramelised onions (page 12)*
*12–16 slices rare roast beef*
*salt flakes*
*freshly ground black pepper*

**1/** Preheat a grill (broiler). Toast both sides of the Turkish bread and place two cheese slices on the inside of all the top slices of bread. Grill (broil) the cheese to melt. Reserve.

**2/** Cover the bottom slices of the Turkish bread with the carrot salad and add four tomatoes per sandwich. Add the caramelised onions followed by the beef slices. Season with salt and pepper and top with the cheesy lids. Heat a toasted sandwich press and cook for 1 minute to press the sandwich flat, then serve.

# Strawberry, prosciutto, manchego ± honey.

**This. Just. Works. Try it – I promise you will love it! Sweet, salty, crunchy and melty.**

### Pro tip
I think the baguette works well, so I would recommend you find a nice one that's not too bready, which will allow these amazing ingredients to sing.

### Makes
4

### Prep time
15 minutes

### Toasting method
**Toasted sandwich press and grill (broiler)**

### Bread
**4 individual baguettes, split, or 1 large baguette, cut into four and sliced lengthways**

*80 ml (2½ fl oz/⅓ cup) olive oil*
*120 g (4½ oz) strawberries, hulled and sliced*
*12 thin slices prosciutto*
*12 thin slices manchego*
*90 g (3 oz/¼ cup) honey*

**1/** Heat a toasted sandwich press. Preheat a chargrill pan or barbecue for 5 minutes to hot. Drizzle some of the olive oil inside the baguettes and place them on the grill or barbecue to char and toast slightly.

**2/** Remove the bread and arrange the slices of strawberry on the baguettes, followed by the prosciutto and manchego. Add 1 tablespoon of honey to each sandwich, close and rub some olive oil on the outside of each baguette. Heat a toasted sandwich press and cook the baguettes for a few minutes until crispy on the outside. Remove, cut in half and serve.

WAIT A SEC...

# Grill.

(SEARED THINGS)

# Two-cheese Welsh rarebit
# w̲ smoked ham ± piccalilli.

What's better than this Welsh rarebit on a Sunday night? Fire on, glass of pinot, a movie and you are set. Sunday night used to be bath night when I was a kid. I reckon Mum and Dad were tucking into a slice or two of this while I was upstairs in the bath.

### Pro tip
I love all cheese but especially cheddar. I love all cheddars but especially Montgomery cheddar. Try and find it if you can, but you'll have to look in special cheese shops or at the market. Any other cheddar will work though, so don't panic.

### Makes
**8 pieces (serves 4)**

### Prep time
**18 minutes (plus chilling)**

### Toasting method
**Grill (broiler)**

### Bread
**8 slices wholemeal sandwich loaf**

35 g (1¼ oz) unsalted butter
35 g (1¼ oz/¼ cup) plain (all-purpose) flour
330 ml (11 fl oz) beer
150 g (5½ oz) Montgomery cheddar, grated
150 g (5½ oz) gruyère, grated
1 teaspoon English mustard
1 teaspoon dijon mustard
1 tablespoon worcestershire sauce
1 egg yolk
salt flakes
freshly ground black pepper
2 tablespoons chopped fresh chives
8–12 slices smoked leg ham
Piccalilli (page 10), to serve

**1/** Melt the butter in a heavy-based saucepan over medium–low heat. (I like to use a cast-iron pan, but any pan will do.) Add the flour and cook, stirring with a heat-resistant spatula, for 3 minutes. Gradually add the beer, whisking the mixture to a smooth paste after every addition. Reduce the heat to low and cook for 3 minutes, stirring constantly with the spatula to stop the mixture from sticking to the pan.

**2/** Remove the pan from the heat, add the cheeses and stir well to incorporate. Add the mustards, worcestershire sauce, egg yolk, salt and pepper and the chives. Whisk well until you have a smooth paste. Transfer the mixture to a plastic container, cover with plastic wrap touching the surface, to stop a skin forming, and chill in the refrigerator for a minimum of 2 hours.

**3/** Preheat a grill (broiler) to hot. Lightly toast the slices of bread on both sides. Spread a tablespoon of the rarebit mixture on one side of each piece of toast and top evenly with the ham. Then spread 2 tablespoons of the rarebit mixture onto the ham. Use a knife or small spatula to try to cover the ham entirely and spread the mixture as close as possible to the edges of the bread.

**4/** Place the slices under the grill and cook the rarebit mixture to an even deep-brown colour, then remove from the grill. Serve immediately, cut in half diagonally, with a side of piccalilli (two pieces of rarebit per person).

# Fried egg ± anchovy toasted sandwich.

Some things just work so well together, and eggs and anchovies are in that category. They are especially good in this posh egg on toast. The anchovy butter is delicious by itself on toast, as well as for many other dishes – try rubbing a chicken with it before roasting!

### Pro tips
Use the best anchovies you can afford. Freshly grated lemon zest will really lift this toast. Any bread works well, but I have opted for a great toasting Turkish, as I love the oil and seeds in the bread.

### Makes
4

### Prep time
18 minutes

### Toasting method
Grill (broiler)

### Bread
four 10 cm (4 in) pieces Turkish bread, cut lengthways

12 anchovy fillets (Ortiz or other good-quality brand)
60 g (2 oz) unsalted butter, softened
freshly ground black pepper
finely grated zest of ¼ lemon
2 tablespoons finely chopped fresh chives
½ teaspoon cayenne pepper
½ teaspoon freshly grated nutmeg
½ teaspoon worcestershire sauce
4 Fried eggs (page 15)
salt flakes
1 handful watercress, plus extra to serve

1/ Preheat a grill (broiler) to hot and toast both sides of the eight pieces of Turkish bread. Chop four of the anchovy fillets finely. Combine these with the butter, pepper, lemon zest, chives, cayenne pepper, nutmeg and worcestershire sauce.

2/ Spread the anchovy butter on four slices of bread and top each one with a fried egg and two anchovy fillets. Arrange some of the watercress on top and close the sandwiches with the remaining slices of toast. Using a serrated knife, push down gently and cut the sandwiches in half. Serve immediately with more fresh watercress.

# Avocado, vegemite ± lime toast w̲ tamari seeds.

Does the world need another shot of avo toast? Yup! My Sunday breakfast of choice, this is the best. I used to prefer Marmite when I was living in the UK, but I am now converted to Vegemite. It doesn't rip my toast and has a milder flavour, which I think works better with the avocado. I suppose you could use your preference of yeasty spread – just don't come running to me when your toast rips.

**Pro tip**
The tamari seeds are a fantastic crunchy addition and are great in salads and as a snack on their own. I adapted the recipe from the original by Aussie wholefood chef and author Jude Blereau.

**Makes**
4

**Prep time**
10 minutes

**Toasting method**
Grill (broiler)

**Bread**
one 30 cm (12 in) long
Turkish loaf

*80 g (2¾ oz) unsalted butter,*
*at room temperature*
*Vegemite to taste*
*2 avocados*
*freshly ground black pepper*
*80 g (2¾ oz) Tamari seeds*
*(page 2)*
*½ lime*

**1/** Preheat a grill (broiler) to hot. Cut the Turkish loaf in half lengthways. Cut both pieces through the middle to leave you with four flat, 15 cm (6 in) long pieces of bread. Toast both sides of the bread under the hot grill.

**2/** Spread the butter on each slice of bread and then apply Vegemite to taste (I like mine thick).

**3/** Cut the avocados in half, discard the stone and peel. Cut each half into slices and arrange a half on each slice of toast. Top with the black pepper and tamari seeds and use a microplane to grate the lime zest onto each slice, then squeeze the juice of the lime half over the top. Serve.

# My cheese on toast w̲ chorizo, tomato, chilli ± ~~cilantro~~ coriander.

**Hi, my name's Darren and I'm a cheese-on-toast-aholic. I eat it around once a week. I've lost control. I need help getting my life back.**

### Pro tip
I developed the double-layer grilling technique over a long period of many Sunday nights of research. I give you…my life's work. *Takes a bow*

### Makes
4

### Prep time
25 minutes

### Toasting method
Grill (broiler)

### Bread
8 slices soy and linseed sourdough loaf

1 dried chorizo sausage, peeled and sliced 5 mm (¼ in) thick
120 g (4½ oz) gruyère, grated
4 ripe truss tomatoes, halved and flesh and seeds scooped out
4 spring onions (scallions), white part only, thinly sliced
80 g (2¾ oz) mozzarella, torn into chunks
140 g (5 oz) Montgomery cheddar, grated
60 ml (2 fl oz/¼ cup) worcestershire sauce
a few drops of sriracha sauce (see page 159) or other similiar hot chilli sauce
120 g (4½ oz) Meredith marinated goat's cheese, crumbled
freshly ground black pepper
½ bunch fresh coriander (cilantro), leaves picked

**1/** Preheat a grill (broiler) to hot. Cook the chorizo slices in a saucepan over medium heat for a few minutes on each side. Leave the chorizo in the pan to cool.

**2/** Lightly toast the eight slices of bread and place them on a baking tray lined with baking paper.

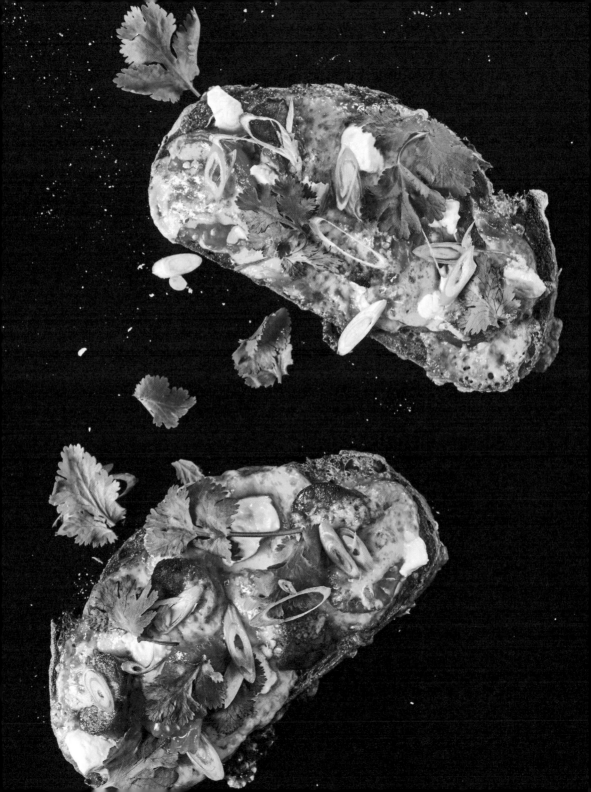

**3/** Evenly distribute the gruyère on each slice of toast, then add the chorizo slices. (Reserve the chorizo oil in the pan.) Place the tray under the grill and melt the cheese.

**4/** Remove the tray from the grill and add the tomato flesh and seeds followed by the spring onion. Again place the tray under the grill and cook for a minute or two to warm the ingredients and start to brown the cheese.

**5/** Remove the tray from the grill and add the torn mozzarella and grated cheddar to each slice. Add the worcestershire sauce, sriracha sauce and spoon the chorizo oil from the pan over the cheese. Again place the tray under the grill and cook to melt and brown the cheese on the toast. Remove from the grill, add the crumbled goat's cheese, pepper and coriander leaves and serve.

# Roast chicken w̲ lemon, thyme ± oregano whipped nut butter.

This toasted sandwich could be constructed from the left-over chicken from a roast but I actually roast a chicken just for this sandwich. Very naughty – crispy skin, lots of salt and loads of nutty butter. At least it's on wholemeal bread!

### Pro tip
There's a bit of work in the butter recipe, but give it a go as it whips up a treat. If you make the butter first, you can use the excess to roast the chicken in as well.

### Makes
4

### Prep time
10 minutes (plus chilling)

### Toasting method
Grill (broiler)

### Bread
8 slices wholemeal sandwich loaf

250 g (9 oz) unsalted butter, softened
finely grated zest of ½ lemon
4 tablespoons chopped fresh oregano leaves
2 teaspoons chopped fresh thyme leaves
salt flakes
4 cos (romaine) lettuce leaves
1 whole roast chicken, skin on
freshly ground black pepper

**1/** Combine the butter with the lemon zest, oregano, thyme and salt and mix well with a spoon or spatula. Cover and store in the refrigerator overnight.

**2/** Place the chilled flavoured butter in a small saucepan over medium–low heat to gently melt it. Continue to cook the butter to 'noisette' stage, or until it is a lightly toasted, nutty brown colour. Remove the pan from the heat. Strain the butter through a sieve into a plastic container and store, covered, in the refrigerator for a minimum of 4 hours until set.

**3/** Remove the butter from the refrigerator and transfer it to the bowl of a freestanding electric mixer fitted with the whisk. Whip the butter on medium speed until you have a smooth and light consistency.

**4/** Preheat a grill (broiler) to hot. Toast the slices of bread under the grill. Generously spread some of the whipped butter on one side of each slice of toast. Place the lettuce leaves on four of the slices. Add the chicken pieces cut from the bird to each slice – I like half a breast and a bit of leg meat – and season with salt and pepper. Close the sandwich, cut in half and serve immediately.

# Toasted baguette w̲ scrambled egg ± harissa.

**Some of the best things are the simplest! Absolute heaven, this is comfort food that you will go back to again and again.**

### Pro tips
Any soft cheese will do for melting into your eggs. I love this goat's cheese, but you could switch to a mozzarella or burrata, camembert or a young fontina. Don't forget to make a big batch of harissa and freeze it in ice cube trays for a quick and convenient spice kick to your dishes through the coming months.

### Makes
4

### Prep time
15 minutes

### Toasting method
Grill (broiler)

### Bread
4 individual baguettes, sliced lengthways (but don't cut all the way through)

60 g (2 oz) unsalted butter
2 tablespoons light olive oil
8 eggs, lightly beaten
salt flakes
freshly ground black pepper
80 g (2¾ oz) Meredith marinated goat's cheese
2 tablespoons chopped fresh coriander (cilantro) leaves
Harissa (page 2)

**1/** Preheat a grill (broiler) to hot. Toast the insides of the baguettes under the grill, then set aside.

**2/** Heat a non-stick frying pan over low heat and add the butter and oil followed by the eggs, salt and pepper. Cook the eggs slowly, stirring occasionally with a spatula, until you have just-set scrambled eggs.

**3/** Remove the eggs from the heat and crumble the goat's cheese over them and add the coriander. Stir to combine. Fill the baguettes with the egg mixture and add harissa to taste.

# Spicy fried chicken roll
# <u>w</u> coleslaw ± pickles.

**A ridiculously naughty fried chicken bun with my special blend of herbs and spices and crunchy batter that will sort you right out.**

<u>**Pro tip**</u>
The brioche bun is the way to go here – something soft and slightly sweet.

<u>**Makes**</u>
**4**

<u>**Prep time**</u>
**30 minutes**

<u>**Toasting method**</u>
**Grill (broiler)**

<u>**Bread**</u>
**4 sesame seed brioche buns**

4 boneless chicken thighs, cut
    into two even-sized pieces
2 tablespoons salt flakes, plus
    ½ teaspoon
4 tablespoons Mayonnaise
    (page 2), or use store-bought
    Kewpie mayonnaise
1 tablespoon sriracha sauce
    (see page 159) or other
    similar hot chilli sauce
200 g (7 oz/1⅓ cups) plain
    (all-purpose) flour
140 g (5 oz/2⅓ cups) panko
    breadcrumbs
3 teaspoons smoked paprika
3 teaspoons cayenne pepper
1 teaspoon onion powder
½ teaspoon garlic powder
½ teaspoon cumin seeds,
    lightly toasted and ground
½ teaspoon dried oregano
½ teaspoon ground white
    pepper
250 ml (8½ fl oz/1 cup)
    buttermilk
1 litre (34 fl oz/4 cups) canola
    or sunflower oil for frying
200 g (7 oz) Coleslaw (page 13)
4 Dill pickles (page 9), sliced in
    half lengthways
40 g (1½ oz) jalapeños from
    a jar, drained

**1/** Place the chicken pieces in a saucepan and cover with cold water. Add the 2 tablespoons of salt to the pan and bring to a gentle boil over medium heat. Simmer the chicken for 5 minutes before turning the heat off. Leave the chicken in the pan for a further 5 minutes and then remove the meat with tongs and dry it on paper towel. Place the chicken in the refrigerator to cool completely.

**2/** Combine the mayonnaise and sriracha sauce in a bowl. Reserve.

**3/** Combine the flour, breadcrumbs, spices, herbs, white pepper and ½ teaspoon salt flakes in a bowl. Mix well and set aside. Pour the buttermilk into a bowl.

**4/** Coat one piece of chicken at a time by rolling the thigh pieces first in the dry ingredients – making sure you cover the chicken completely – then lifting the chicken to shake off the excess. Dip the chicken in the buttermilk and then place it back in the dry ingredients to cover again. Transfer the chicken to a rack or plate and repeat with the remaining chicken pieces.

**5/** Heat the oil in a deep saucepan to 190°C (375°F), using a thermometer to check the temperature. Fry two pieces of chicken at a time for around 5 minutes, or until you have a crisp and golden-brown crust. Remove the chicken pieces carefully with tongs and reserve them on a rack in a warm oven while you cook the remaining pieces.

**6/** Preheat a grill (broiler) to hot. Cut the buns in half and toast the insides. Spread some of the spicy mayonnaise on the bottom half of each bun, then place two pieces of chicken on top. Add the coleslaw, pickles and jalapeños to each sandwich and top with another dollop of mayonnaise. Top with the bun lid and press down gently.

# Grilled sardines on toast w̲ romesco sauce ± parmesan.

I love sardines. They are great for you, full of omega 3 fatty acid and vitamin D, and they are delish – especially on my favourite vehicle for food…toast! The Romesco sauce (page 9) is quality as well. I guess with this one I am recreating a childhood memory of tinned sardines in tomato sauce on toast. This is better, though. It's quick, simple, healthy and delicious.

### Pro tips
See your fishmonger for fresh sardine fillets. I have used a great toasting sourdough here.

### Makes
4

### Prep time
20 minutes

### Toasting method
Grill (broiler)

### Bread
4 slices seeded sourdough loaf

4 tablespoons Romesco sauce (page 9)
4 small, ripe truss tomatoes
splash of olive oil
8 sardine fillets, butterflied and bones removed
40 g (1½ oz) Parmigiano Reggiano
freshly ground black pepper
½ lemon
½ bunch fresh flat-leaf (Italian) parsley, leaves picked, to serve

**1/** Preheat a grill (broiler) to hot. Toast both sides of the bread under the grill. Spread a tablespoon of romesco on each piece of toast. Cut the tomatoes in half, scoop the flesh and seeds out and place them on top of the romesco.

**2/** Heat a splash of olive oil in a small non-stick frying pan over medium–low heat and gently cook the sardine fillets, skin side down, for 2 minutes. Remove from the heat and use a spatula or fish slice to arrange two butterflied sardine fillets on each piece of toast.

**3/** Place the slices on a baking tray lined with baking paper and place the tray under the grill for 1 minute before removing and grating the parmesan over the top of each slice. Again place the tray back under the grill and cook for 2 minutes to melt the cheese. Remove again and grind black pepper over each slice and finely grate lemon zest over the top. Place the toast on a plate, top with the parsley leaves and serve.

# Curried ~~lobster~~ crayfish roll w̲ mango chutney ± potato chips.

A shout out to all past pupils at Park Barn Comprehensive School in Guildford, UK – later named Kings Manor. A favourite lunch enjoyed by many of us at this fine institution was prawn cocktail-flavoured potato chips (crisps) – just 15 pence – in a buttered white bread roll (5 pence). It was really all a growing kid needed and I have loved chips in my sandwiches ever since. This is my all-grown-up version.

## Pro tips
Fresh seafood in mayo is one of life's great pleasures. Try preparing your own crayfish, following the instructions in the method, or visit a decent fishmonger for some prepared meat. Again a brioche bun here is the way forward and the surprise of mango chutney really takes this to the next level.

## Makes
**4**

## Prep time
**10 minutes (if using prepared crayfish meat)**

## Toasting method
**Grill (broiler)**

## Bread
**4 seeded brioche buns**

1 × 1.5 kg (3 lb 5 oz) live crayfish, or 500 g (1 lb 2 oz) crayfish meat, chopped into large chunks
salt flakes
iced water
120 g (4½ oz) Mayonnaise (page 2), or use store-bought Kewpie mayonnaise
2 teaspoons curry powder
2 celery stalks, sliced
½ cucumber, peeled, seeded and cut into 1 cm (½ in) dice
1 tablespoon finely shredded fresh mint leaves
freshly ground black pepper
8 cos (romaine) lettuce leaves, shredded
4 tablespoons Mango chutney (page 8)
Potato chips (page 15), to serve

**1/** If using prepared crayfish flesh, skip to step 3. If using a live crayfish, follow these instructions. Place the crayfish in the freezer for 45 minutes. Remove the crayfish from the freezer and, using a sharp, sturdy knife, split the crayfish lengthways through the head.

**2/** Bring a large saucepan of heavily salted water to the boil and add the crayfish. Cook for 18–20 minutes until it's bright orange in colour. Remove from the heat and drain the water. Use a couple of tea towels (dish towels) to help you grip the crayfish as you separate the tail from the head by twisting and pulling them in opposite directions. Plunge the crayfish into a large bowl of iced water. Once cool, remove it and use kitchen scissors to cut the underside of the tail to release and remove the tail meat intact. Cut out and discard the intestinal tract. Cut the flesh into large chunks and place it in a bowl.

**3/** Combine the mayonnaise with the curry powder, celery, cucumber, shredded mint and salt and pepper. Mix well and fold in the cooked crayfish meat.

**4/** Preheat a grill (broiler) to hot. Cut the buns all the way through the middle and open them out. Toast them on the insides and then stuff them with shredded lettuce before adding a tablespoon of mango chutney to each. Spoon the crayfish filling evenly into the buns and push it in well. Stuff potato chips into the buns and serve.

KEEN'S

TRADITIONAL

CURRY
POWDER

120g

# Peanut butter, cheesy omelette ± BLT toasted bagel.

A huge thanks to talented pastry chef Nicole Liao – or Gin, as we call her – for showing me this neat cheese-wrapped-in-omelette technique, and for convincing me to try the surprising but delicious combo of peanut butter and a BLT. Who would have thought!

## Pro tips
I've gone for a toasted sesame seed bagel here, which is just the right size to hold all of this together. Just a thin scraping of peanut butter will do to add a new dimension to this sandwich. The omelette is a great trick up any sandwich aficionado's sleeve.

## Makes
4

## Prep time
13 minutes

## Toasting method
Grill (broiler)

## Bread
4 bagels

60 g (2 oz) unsalted butter, softened
60 g (2 oz) peanut butter
4 baby gem lettuce leaves, washed
8 cold-smoked bacon rashers (slices)
2 small, ripe truss tomatoes, thinly sliced
salt flakes
freshly ground black pepper
1 Cheesy omelette square (page 15)

**1/** Preheat a grill (broiler) to hot. Cut the bagels in half and toast them under the grill.

**2/** Butter the bagels and thinly spread the peanut butter evenly on the bottom halves. Place the lettuce leaves on the peanut butter, then the bacon, followed by the tomato slices. Season the slices with salt and pepper and add the cheesy omelette square on top. Close the bagels with the top halves and serve immediately.

# Christmas Day left-over club melt: turkey, brie, cranberry, bacon ± stuffing.

**Knock this up on Christmas Day evening or Boxing Day anytime to keep the party going. The hardest part of this sandwich is to cook a couple of rashers of bacon. If you don't do turkey round your house for Christmas, then use ham, pork, chicken, goose, beef or whatever instead. Press down on this triple-decker or it will topple over quicker than Nan after a few sherries. This melt's what Jesus would have wanted on his birthday.**

<u>**Pro tips**</u>
Avocado is a great fresh element and is a natural playmate of bacon. This sandwich is potentially the best use of a turkey.

<u>**Makes**</u>
4

<u>**Prep time**</u>
20 minutes

<u>**Toasting method**</u>
Grill (broiler)

<u>**Bread**</u>
12 slices sourdough loaf

12 slices brie, rind cut off
60 g (2 oz) unsalted butter, softened
120 g (4½ oz) stuffing, at room temperature
12 slices turkey, left over from the roast
160 ml (5½ fl oz) gravy or jus, left over from the roast
4 tablespoons cranberry sauce
8 rashers (slices) bacon, cooked
1 avocado, peeled and sliced
salt flakes
freshly ground black pepper

**1/** Preheat a grill (broiler) to hot. Toast all twelve slices of bread under the grill. Add the brie to four of the bread slices. Place them under the grill to melt the cheese, then remove and set aside.

**2/** Butter four slices of the remaining toast. Working butter side up, spread the stuffing over each slice. Arrange slices of turkey on top and add a spoonful or so of gravy to moisten the meat. Add cranberry sauce and top with the slices of melted brie toast, cheese side up. Add the bacon rashers on top of the cheese and then the sliced avocado. Season with salt and pepper and top with the remaining piece of toast. Press down gently and serve.

# Iron.

(SEALED THINGS)

CALLED A 'JAFFLE' IN AUSTRALIA AND A CLASSIC SINCE 1949, COOKED USING A PIE (SANDWICH) IRON - ALL THE YUMMY THINGS ARE SEALED INSIDE.

IN THE UK, SOME FOLKS CALL IT A 'BREVILLE'.

# Mac ± cheese jaffle.

**Carb-ageddon has finally arrived! The cheeses here are just a suggestion, but you can try your own combinations.**

## Pro tips

I tried this with many different breads and have come to the conclusion that only supermarket white sandwich will do for this one. Load it up with cheese for that extra gooey centre. This is a great use of left-over pasta and why stop here? Spaghetti bolognese jaffle anyone?

## Makes
4

## Prep time
40 minutes (plus standing)

## Toasting method
Pie (sandwich) iron

## Bread
8 slices white sandwich loaf

½ brown onion
1 clove
600 ml (20½ fl oz) full-cream (whole) milk
25 g (1 oz) unsalted butter, softened, plus extra for spreading on the bread
25 g (1 oz) plain (all-purpose) flour
150 g (5½ oz) gruyère, grated
150 g (5½ oz) young fontina, grated
2 tablespoons finely chopped fresh chives
1 tablespoon white-wine vinegar
salt flakes
white pepper
freshly grated nutmeg
250 g (9 oz) small elbow macaroni or mini tubes
180 g (6½ oz) comté, grated

**1/** Place the onion, clove and milk in a saucepan over medium heat and bring to the boil. Remove from the heat and leave to infuse for 30 minutes. Bring back to the boil and strain the hot milk into a jug.

**2/** Melt the butter in a heavy-based saucepan over medium–low heat. (I like to use a cast-iron pan, but any pan will do.) Add the flour and cook, stirring with a heat-resistant spatula, for 3 minutes. Slowly add the strained milk in four stages, whisking the mixture to a smooth paste after every addition. Reduce the heat to low and cook for 10 minutes, stirring constantly with the spatula to stop the mixture from sticking to the pan. Remove the pan from the heat, add the gruyère and fontina and stir well to incorporate. Mix in the chives, vinegar and season with salt, pepper and nutmeg. Set aside in a warm place.

YASSSSSSSS

**3/** Bring a medium saucepan of salted water to the boil and add the macaroni. Cook following the packet instructions or until al dente, then drain.

**4/** Add the cooked macaroni to the cheese sauce and stir it in well. Leave the mixture to cool – if it gets too thick, you can add a splash of warm milk, but remember it will loosen once reheated.

**5/** Preheat a pie (sandwich) iron. Butter one side of each slice of bread. Assemble your four sandwiches directly in the pie iron (two at a time if that is the size of your machine). Place four slices of bread, butter side down, in the pie iron and spoon 2–3 heaped tablespoons of macaroni cheese in the centre of the slices. Top with a quarter of the grated comté. Close the sandwiches with the remaining slices of bread, buttered side up. Finish all four sandwiches and then cook them in the pie iron until they are golden brown and sealed.

# Cheesy polenta, wild mushrooms ± thyme jaffle.

The buttery, herb-infused mushrooms are so delicious in this jaffle. Some things just go together and mushrooms, butter, herbs and cheesy polenta are some of those things.

## Pro tips

Use whatever mushrooms you prefer in this and, likewise, change the cheese if you prefer something else or can't find fontina. Raclette works as well. This will make more polenta than you need, so it's a great way of using up polenta from last night's dinner or getting ahead for tomorrow night's dinner.

## Makes
4

## Prep time
30 minutes (plus cooling)

## Toasting method
Pie (sandwich) iron

## Bread
8 slices white sandwich loaf

750 ml (25½ fl oz/3 cups) full-cream (whole) milk
125 g (4½ oz) polenta
100 g (3½ oz) unsalted butter, plus extra for spreading
60 g (2 oz) Parmigiano Reggiano, finely grated
1 tablespoon finely chopped fresh tarragon leaves
1 tablespoon finely chopped fresh chives
100 g (3½ oz) young fontina, chopped into cubes
salt flakes
freshly ground black pepper
60 ml (2 fl oz/¼ cup) light olive oil
100 g (3½ oz) shiitake mushrooms, thickly sliced
100 g (3½ oz) Swiss brown mushrooms, thickly sliced
100 g (3½ oz) oyster mushrooms, thickly sliced
4 portobello mushrooms, thickly sliced
1 tablespoon chopped fresh thyme leaves
1 tablespoon worcestershire sauce
juice of ¼ lemon

1/ Place the milk in a large cast-iron or heavy-bottomed saucepan over medium heat and bring to a simmer. Whisk in the polenta in a steady stream. Reduce the heat to low and cook the polenta for 10 minutes, whisking constantly. When the polenta is smooth and cooked through, whisk in half the butter, followed by the Parmigiano Reggiano. Fold in the herbs and finally stir in the fontina until melted. Remove from the heat and season to taste before covering the polenta in the pan with plastic wrap that is touching the surface, to ensure a skin does not form. Set aside.

2/ Heat the oil in a large non-stick frying pan over high heat and add the sliced mushrooms and thyme. Cook for 5 minutes until the mushrooms are golden and soft. Season with salt and pepper and cook for a further minute. Remove the mushrooms from the pan and add the remaining butter to the pan. Place the pan back on the heat and cook the butter to 'noisette' stage – until the butter turns brown and smells nutty. Remove the pan from the heat and add the worcestershire sauce and lemon juice. Return the mushrooms to the pan and toss again to mix. Remove the pan from the heat and set aside.

3/ Preheat a pie (sandwich) iron. Butter one side of each of the slices of bread. Assemble your four sandwiches directly in the pie iron (two at a time if that is the size of your machine). Place the bread slices, butter side down, in the pie iron and spread a generous amount of polenta on top. Add some mushrooms and sauce and top the jaffle with another slice of bread, butter side up. Close the pie iron and cook until golden brown and sealed.

# Spicy lamb mince jaffle <u>w</u> soft labne spread.

This lamb comes from a borek recipe from my wife, Cath, who is a Middle Eastern food expert. It's easy to make, delicious and the pine nuts are a great addition. The spices and herbs are added last to keep things fresh.

### Pro tips
Labne is simple to make. It's so good rolled into balls, coated in chopped herbs or dukkah and used on a mezze plate. It is used here as a sort of dip, or spread, for the lamb jaffles.

### Makes
4

### Prep time
45 minutes (plus draining and cooling)

### Toasting method
Pie (sandwich) iron

### Bread
8 slices white sandwich loaf

500 g (1 lb 2 oz) Greek-style yoghurt
1 teaspoon salt flakes
1 brown onion, finely diced
1 bird's eye chilli, seeded and chopped
2 garlic cloves, grated
50 ml (1¾ fl oz) light olive oil
500 g (1 lb 2 oz) minced (ground) lamb
1 tablespoon tomato paste (concentrated purée)
500 ml (17 fl oz/2 cups) chicken stock
50 g (1¾ oz/⅓ cup) pine nuts, toasted
1 teaspoon cayenne pepper
1 teaspoon allspice
3 tablespoons chopped fresh coriander (cilantro) leaves
1 tablespoon chopped fresh flat-leaf (Italian) parsley leaves
80 g (2¾ oz) unsalted butter, softened

**1/** Make the labne a day ahead. Mix the yoghurt with the salt and pour it into a sieve lined with muslin (cheesecloth) set over a plastic container. Leave to hang overnight to extract all of the whey. Transfer the thick labne to a plastic container and store in the refrigerator until needed. Discard the whey.

**2/** In a large cast-iron or heavy-based saucepan, gently fry the onion, chilli and garlic in the oil for a few minutes over medium heat until translucent. Raise the heat to medium–high and add the lamb. Brown it off and mix with a wooden spoon until all the juices have evaporated. Just as the meat starts to catch on the bottom of the saucepan, add the tomato paste and fry for another minute or so. Add the chicken stock to deglaze the pan and stir. Reduce the heat to low and simmer gently for about 10 minutes or until all the liquid has evaporated. Remove from the heat and leave to cool. Add the pine nuts, spices and herbs and mix well.

**3/** Preheat a pie (sandwich) iron. Butter one side of each of the slices of bread. Assemble your four sandwiches directly in the pie iron (two at a time if that is the size of your machine). Place the bread slices, butter side down, in the pie iron and add 3–4 heaped tablespoons of spicy lamb. Spread to just inside the edges of the bread. Top with the remaining slices of bread, buttered side up. Close the pie iron and cook until the sandwiches are golden brown and sealed. Serve with the labne as a spread.

# Baked bean jaffle.

**This is probably one of the most iconic jaffles of our time. Critics have lauded its simplistic design and complex taste, Darling. Mwah!**

### Pro tip
What? Of course you can use a tin of baked beans! I just thought you might like to make your own. Calm down.

### Makes
**4**

### Prep time
**3½ hours (plus soaking and cooling)**

### Toasting method
**Pie (sandwich) iron**

### Bread
**8 slices white sandwich loaf**

*350 g (12½ oz) dried haricot beans*
*3 tablespoons olive oil*
*3 brown onions, chopped*
*3 garlic cloves, chopped*
*1 carrot, cut into 5 mm (¼ in) dice*
*2 teaspoons smoked paprika*
*½ teaspoon ground cloves*
*2 tablespoons tomato paste (concentrated purée)*
*500 ml (17 fl oz/2 cups) tomato passata (puréed tomatoes)*
*1 teaspoon chopped fresh thyme leaves*
*1 bay leaf*
*1 tablespoon worcestershire sauce*
*20 g (¾ oz) soft brown sugar*
*salt flakes*
*freshly ground black pepper*
*80 g (2¾ oz) unsalted butter*
*120 g (4½ oz) cheddar, grated*

**1/** Soak the dried beans in plenty of cold water for 12 hours. Drain the beans and discard the water. Preheat the oven to 150°C (300°F).

**2/** Rinse the beans well before placing them in a large saucepan. Cover the beans with cold water and bring to the boil over medium heat. Turn off the heat and leave the beans in the pan to cool, then drain the water. Rinse the beans in cold water, then drain again.

**3/** Heat the oil in a large cast-iron pan or flameproof casserole over medium heat and sauté the onion, garlic and carrot. Cook for 5 minutes until the vegetables are soft and golden. Sprinkle the paprika and ground cloves over the vegetables and cook for a further minute.

**4/** Add the tomato paste and stir it through before adding the beans, passata, thyme, bay leaf, worcestershire sauce and sugar. Stir well until the mixture gently comes to the boil. Season with salt and pepper. Add 350 ml (12 fl oz) water and place a lid on the pan.

**5/** Transfer the pan to the oven and cook for 2 hours. Remove the pan from the oven and stir well. Check the seasoning again and, if the mixture looks too dry, add some water to thin it out. Replace the lid, return the pan to the oven and cook for a further 1½ hours. Remove from the oven and allow the mixture to cool to a thick and rich sauce. Store the beans in a container in the refrigerator until needed.

**6/** Preheat a pie (sandwich) iron. Butter one side of each of the slices of bread. Assemble your four sandwiches directly in the pie (sandwich) iron (two at a time if that is the size of your machine). Place the bread slices, butter side down, in the pie iron and add 2 heaped tablespoons of the baked bean mixture in the centre and top with a quarter of the grated cheese. Top with the remaining slices of bread, buttered side up. Close the pie iron and cook until golden brown and sealed.

AN ORIGINAL!!!

# Roasted cauliflower cheese jaffle w̲ fresh truffle.

How luxe is this? I love regular cauliflower cheese, but the fresh truffle sends this humble jaffle into the premier league.

## Pro tips
I have gone for brioche here, as the recipe is decadent and luxurious. But you could use straight white sandwich bread as well. Try to find some truffles from your local market. They can be expensive, but a little goes a very long way.

## Makes
4

## Prep time
50 minutes (plus cooling)

## Toasting method
Pie (sandwich) iron

## Bread
8 thin slices brioche loaf

1 cauliflower
60 ml (2 fl oz/¼ cup) light
    olive oil
salt flakes
freshly ground black pepper
1 teaspoon white-wine vinegar
120 g (4½ oz) unsalted butter
2 French shallots, finely
    chopped
2 fresh thyme sprigs, leaves
    picked and chopped
1 bay leaf
25 g (1 oz) plain (all-purpose)
    flour
300 ml (10 fl oz) full-cream
    (whole) milk, warmed
200 ml (7 fl oz) thickened
    (whipping) cream
1 tablespoon dijon mustard
1 teaspoon horseradish sauce
350 g (12½ oz) comté or
    gruyère, grated
150 g (5½ oz) taleggio, sliced
1 tablespoon finely chopped
    fresh chives
salad leaves, to serve
Vinaigrette (page 3), to serve
freshly sliced truffle, to serve
    (optional)

**1/** Cut the cauliflower into small florets using a small knife. Set half aside and thinly slice the remaining florets. Cut any stem pieces to roughly the same size as the florets and add them to the first batch of florets.

**2/** Preheat the oven to 180°C (350°F). Toss the second batch of florets in half the olive oil, season them with salt and pepper and spread these evenly on a baking tray. Bake for approximately 20–25 minutes, stirring from time to time to ensure the cauliflower browns evenly. When ready, the florets should be tinged golden brown on the edges and be completely tender. Remove from the oven and set aside.

**3/** Bring a medium saucepan of salted water (with the vinegar added) to the boil. Add the remaining florets and stem pieces. Blanch for 2 minutes, then remove from the heat. Drain the water but keep the florets hot.

**4/** Heat 40 g (1½ oz) of the butter with the remaining oil in a cast-iron or heavy-based saucepan over low heat. Add the shallots, thyme, a pinch of salt and the bay leaf. Cook for a couple of minutes until the shallots are translucent. Add another 40 g (1½ oz) of the butter and the flour and cook for 1 minute before adding the milk and cream. Mix well, then add the mustard, horseradish and the blanched florets and stem. Reduce the heat to low and cook for a further 5 minutes to thicken, stirring regularly. Add the cheeses and cook for a further 2 minutes, stirring often. Season if needed with salt and pepper.

**5/** Transfer the entire contents of the pan to a blender. Blitz to a smooth cheesy cauliflower sauce, then scrape the sauce into a bowl. Fold through the roasted cauliflower pieces and the chives, cover with plastic wrap and allow the sauce to cool at room temperature before using.

**6/** Preheat a pie (sandwich) iron. Butter one side of each slice of bread. Assemble your four sandwiches directly in the pie (sandwich) iron (two at a time if that is the size of your machine). Place the bottom slices of bread, butter side down, in the pie iron. Place 3 heaped tablespoons of cauliflower cheese mix into the centre of the bread, then top with the remaining slices of bread, buttered side up. Close the pie iron and cook for a few minutes until golden brown and sealed. Serve with salad leaves dressed in vinaigrette and sliced truffle over the top, if desired.

# Pan.

(FRIED THINGS)

# Bulgarian feta, caramelised onion, lemon ± mint in chive egg batter.

This is cheesy, zesty and fresh. It's battered but light at the same time and that's down to the fluffy brioche. The caramelised onions (page 12), which are cooked in the microwave, are ridiculous and would go well in any sandwich in this book. Get onto them....now!

### Pro tips
The tangy feta goes well with the zesty lemon and fresh mint. The cheddar melts it all together and the added parmesan is a great carrier of flavour. Soft-style bread is essential to soak up the egg batter.

### Makes
4

### Prep time
20 minutes

### Toasting method
Pan and oven

### Bread
8 slices brioche loaf

150 g (5½ oz) Bulgarian feta, crumbled
175 g (6 oz) mature cheddar, grated
10 fresh mint leaves, finely shredded
finely grated zest of 1 lemon
freshly ground black pepper
160 g (5½ oz) Caramelised onions (page 12)
180 g (6½ oz) unsalted butter

*Chive egg batter*
3 eggs
150 ml (5 fl oz) full-cream (whole) milk
40 g (1½ oz) Parmigiano Reggiano
4 tablespoons chopped fresh chives
freshly ground black pepper

**1/** Preheat the oven to 180°C (350°F). For the chive egg batter, mix all the ingredients together in a bowl. Set aside.

**2/** Mix the feta and cheddar together in a bowl and add the mint, lemon zest and pepper. Evenly distribute the cheese mix between four slices of brioche, pushing the filling to the edges and evenly levelling it off. Evenly distribute the caramelised onion on top of the cheese. Close the sandwiches with the remaining brioche slices and gently press down.

**3/** Heat a non-stick frying pan over medium heat, add half the butter and let it melt. Briefly dip two of the sandwiches in the chive egg batter on both sides. Place the sandwiches in the pan and cook them for 4–5 minutes. Use a spatula to gently flip each sandwich over and cook for a further 4 minutes. Use the spatula to transfer the sandwiches to a baking tray lined with baking paper. Wipe the frying pan with paper towel and repeat the steps for the remaining two sandwiches.

**4/** Transfer the baking tray to the oven and cook the sandwiches for a further 6 minutes. Remove from the oven and leave them to sit for a minute before cutting them in half and serving immediately.

# Croque monsieur <u>w</u> tarragon, sweet mustard salad ± mango chutney.

**A classic for a reason, this sandwich can be found on menus all over the world. But how many are not up to scratch? This is as comforting as a hug from Nan. The tarragon vinegar and fresh tarragon make this sandwich spectacular. The mango chutney may seem like an odd pairing, but it really works. And a sweet mustard salad is the perfect addition.**

## Pro tips
Switch gruyère for any other melty cheese, like emmental or cheddar, if you prefer. Add a Fried egg (page 15) on top of the sandwich and you have a croque madame! Ooh la la. Left-over béchamel can be used for making additional sandwiches, which can then be frozen. The béchamel can be stored in the refrigerator for up to 4 days, or frozen, and used for pasta bake dishes.

## Makes
**4**

## Prep time
**50 minutes (plus standing and chilling)**

## Toasting method
**Pan and oven**

## Bread
**8 slices brioche loaf**

500 ml (17 fl oz/2 cups) full-cream (whole) milk
½ brown onion
1 clove
125 g (4½ oz) unsalted butter, softened
25 g (1 oz) plain (all-purpose) flour
100 g (3½ oz) dijon mustard
500 g (1 lb 2 oz) gruyère, grated
3 tablespoons chopped fresh tarragon leaves
1 tablespoon tarragon vinegar
salt flakes
freshly ground black pepper
16 slices smoked leg ham
Mango chutney (page 8), to serve

**1/** To make the tarragon béchamel, place the milk, onion and clove in a saucepan over medium heat and bring to the boil. Remove from the heat and leave to infuse for 30 minutes. Return the pan to the stove top, bring back to the boil, then strain the hot milk into a jug.

**2/** In a heavy-based saucepan (I like to use a cast–iron pan, but any pan will do) over medium–low heat, melt 25 g (1 oz) of the butter. Add the flour and cook, stirring with a heat-resistant spatula, for 3 minutes. Slowly add the strained milk in four stages, whisking the mixture to a smooth paste after each addition. Reduce the heat to low and cook for 10 minutes, stirring constantly with the spatula to stop the mixture from sticking to the pan.

**3/** Remove the pan from the heat and add the mustard and 150 g (5½ oz) of the cheese. Stir well to incorporate. Mix in the chopped tarragon and tarragon vinegar and season with salt and pepper. Transfer the mixture to a plastic container, cover with plastic wrap touching the surface to stop a skin forming, and chill in the refrigerator for a minimum of 2 hours.

**4/** Butter four slices of brioche and turn them over. Build the sandwiches, butter side down, on four squares of baking paper for ease of movement. Liberally spread the tarragon béchamel on the brioche slices and spread it to the edges. You will have more béchamel than you need, so don't use too much or the sandwich will go sloppy – about 1 heaped tablespoon per sandwich is enough. Top evenly with the remaining cheese. Grind pepper over each sandwich and top with the ham. Butter the remaining four slices of brioche and close the sandwich, butter side down. Press down gently and butter the top slice of brioche.

**5/** Place the sandwiches in the refrigerator for a minimum of 1 hour – this will help set the béchamel. These can be left in the refrigerator for a couple of days, to cook at your convenience, or can even be wrapped and stored in the freezer for up to 1 month. Just defrost them in the refrigerator for a few hours before cooking.

**6/** Preheat the oven to 180°C (350°F). Heat a non-stick frying pan over medium heat. Add the remaining butter to the pan and swirl to melt. Place the sandwiches, two at a time, in the pan and cook for 5 minutes on each side to achieve a golden and crispy exterior.

**7/** Place the sandwiches on a baking tray lined with baking paper. Bake the sandwiches in the oven for 6–8 minutes. Remove from the oven and serve with a side of mango chutney. To serve with a sweet mustard salad, simply dress salad leaves with Sweet mustard dressing (page 3).

# Egg ± anchovy toast w̲ herb salad.

This is a super-neat trick and a great way of cooking an egg inside a piece of bread without overcooking either of them. Again anchovies are paired with egg, and again it's simple but hits the spot. Olive bread is the perfect slice for this toasted piece of heaven.

## Pro tips

There should be more rubbing of hot toasted bread with cut garlic cloves – the world would be a better place. Practise the egg-cooking-in-bread trick. The secret is to have thick slices of bread and to control your temperature. Got to have that runny yolk!

## Makes
4

## Prep time
15 minutes

## Toasting method
Pan

## Bread
**four 3 cm (1¼ in) slices olive bread**

100 g (3½ oz) unsalted butter
4 eggs
2 garlic cloves
12 anchovy fillets (Ortiz or other good-quality brand)
1 lemon
2 tablespoons fresh flat-leaf (Italian) parsley leaves
2 tablespoons dill fronds
2 tablespoons fresh chives, cut into 2 cm (¾ in) pieces
2 tablespoons fresh baby coriander (cilantro) leaves
2 tablespoons fresh baby chervil leaves
Vinaigrette (page 3)
salt flakes
freshly ground black pepper

**1/** Use a 5 cm (2 in) diameter round cutter to cut a hole in the centre of each slice of bread.

**2/** Melt the butter in a non-stick frying pan over medium heat and lightly fry the first side of all four slices of bread for 3–4 minutes. Flip each slice of bread over and crack an egg into the holes in the bread. Cook for 3 minutes before gently flipping the bread over again and cooking for a further minute. The egg should be set but still runny on the inside.

**3/** Cut the garlic cloves in half and rub a half on each side of the bread. Slice the anchovies and arrange them evenly on the bread. Finely grate lemon zest over each slice. Toss the herbs with a little vinaigrette and season with salt and pepper. Arrange the melts on plates and serve with the herb salad.

# Prawn ± sesame toast w̲ spring onion purée.

I have a thing for prawn toast. It reminds me of the takeaway Chinese food I had with my parents and sister when I was younger. Dad liked lemon chicken, Mum liked anything with king prawns, my sister Emma always had special fried rice and barbecued pork rib things, and I loved all of it – but especially prawn toast.

### Pro tips
Cheapish white sandwich bread works well here and the dipping sauce makes for an unusual but delicious accompaniment to the fried toast.

### Makes
4

### Prep time
35 minutes

### Toasting method
Barbecue, pan and oven

### Bread
4 slices white sandwich loaf, crusts cut off, each slice cut into 2 thick fingers

20 spring onions (scallions), white part only
80 ml (2½ fl oz/⅓ cup) light olive oil
250 ml (8½ fl oz/1 cup) chicken stock
½ bunch chives, finely chopped
salt flakes
white pepper
180 ml (6 fl oz) toasted sesame oil
200 g (7 oz) green (raw) king prawns (jumbo shrimp), peeled and deveined
1 tablespoon peeled and finely grated fresh ginger
2 garlic cloves, finely grated
2 bird's eye chillies, seeded and thinly sliced
1 egg white
2 tablespoons soy sauce
1 tablespoon sesame oil
4 tablespoons sesame seeds
1 litre (34 fl oz/4 cups) canola or sunflower oil for frying

**1/** To make the spring onion purée, grill half the spring onions on a hot barbecue or in a cast-iron grill pan to achieve a charred and smoky finish. Remove from the heat, allow them to cool, then chop the onions finely.

**2/** Setting aside a small handful for garnish, slice the remaining raw spring onions thinly.

**3/** Add the olive oil to a saucepan over low heat and gently sauté the sliced spring onions for a few minutes until soft. Add the chicken stock to the pan and cook for a few minutes until most of the liquid has evaporated. Remove from the heat and add the sliced, charred spring onions and half the chopped chives. Season with salt and pepper and transfer the mixture to a blender. Blitz until you have a textured purée, then blend in the sesame oil. Set aside in the refrigerator.

**4/** For the prawn mix, put the prawns, ginger, garlic, one of the chillies, the egg white, soy sauce and sesame oil in a food processor and blitz until you have a smooth mixture. Transfer the mixture to a bowl and add the remaining chives. Stir to mix well.

**5/** Spread the prawn mixture evenly onto the eight fingers of bread. Press the sesame seeds onto the prawn part of each slice and shake off the excess.

**6/** Heat the canola oil in a deep-fryer or deep saucepan to 180°C (350°F), using a thermometer to check the temperature. Fry one toast at a time for around 3–5 minutes or until you have a crisp and golden-brown crust. Remove the toast carefully with tongs and reserve it on a rack in a warm oven while you cook the remaining slices.

**7/** Serve two fingers per person with the spring onion purée and the reserved sliced spring onion and remaining chilli, sliced.

# Comforting old-school cheese melt.

You can get all fancy, but sometimes the simple things are the best. I've been eating this sandwich in one form or another my entire life, and I reckon I will continue to do so forever. Toast. Cheese. Onion. Simple!

### Pro tips
You can use any bread you like and most cheeses also work. There's so little to this sandwich that you can concentrate on the correct browning of toast to melted cheese ratio for ongoing enjoyment.

### Makes
4

### Prep time
22 minutes

### Sandwich toasting method
Pan and oven

### Bread
8 slices brioche loaf

140 g (5 oz) gruyère, grated
140 g (5 oz) Montgomery
   cheddar, grated
4 spring onions (scallions),
   white part only, thinly sliced
60 ml (2 fl oz/¼ cup)
   worcestershire sauce
freshly ground black pepper
240 g (8½ oz) unsalted butter,
   softened

**1/** Mix the two cheeses together in a bowl. Evenly distribute the cheese between four slices of brioche and level it out with your fingers. Add a sliced spring onion to each sandwich and splash worcestershire sauce over the top. Freshly grind some black pepper on each slice, top with the remaining slices of brioche and push down gently.

**2/** Preheat the oven to 180°C (350°F).

**3/** In a large non-stick frying pan over medium heat, warm 80 g (2¾ oz) of the butter until it is just starting to froth. Add two sandwiches to the pan and cook them for a few minutes until they are golden brown, then flip them over and cook the other side for a minute or two. Use a spatula to remove the sandwiches from the pan and transfer them to a baking tray lined with baking paper. Wipe the frying pan with paper towel and add another 80 g (2¾ oz) of butter. Heat the pan again and cook the remaining two sandwiches the same way as the first. Transfer these to the tray with the other sandwiches.

**4/** Spread the remaining butter on top of the sandwiches, then place them in the oven to bake for 6 minutes. Remove the melts from the oven and allow them to sit for a minute before cutting in half and serving.

# Boxing Day melt: glazed ham, mustard, grilled pineapple ± cheddar.

Get out of bed, take painkillers, crack open a beer, get the cricket on, make these, have some wine, go back to bed.

### Pro tips
Ham and pineapple belong together – don't let those up-themselves friends of yours tell you otherwise. The cheddar crust is a revelation – get it into your life.

### Makes
**4**

### Prep time
**26 minutes**

### Toasting method
**Pan**

### Bread
**8 slices white sandwich loaf**

4 pineapple slices, 1 cm (½ in) thick, peeled and core removed
50 g (1¾ oz) icing (confectioners') sugar
120 g (4½ oz) unsalted butter, softened
4 tablespoons dijon mustard
16 slices glazed ham
160 g (5½ oz) Montgomery cheddar, grated
salt flakes
freshly ground black pepper

**1/** Place a non-stick frying pan over medium heat. Dust both sides of the pineapple slices with the icing sugar. Cook the slices of pineapple in the pan for a couple of minutes on each side to caramelise them until golden brown. Remove from the heat and set aside. Clean the pan for the sandwiches.

**2/** Butter four slices of bread and turn them over. Build the sandwiches, butter side down, on four squares of baking paper for ease of movement. Spread 1 tablespoon of mustard on the bread and add the slices of ham. Evenly distribute half the cheddar on the four slices, then add a pineapple slice. Season with salt and pepper and top with the remaining slice of bread. Butter the top side of the sandwich.

**3/** Divide the remaining cheese into four equal-sized portions. Push half a quantity of cheese into the top slice of bread and repeat with the remaining cheese on both sides of each sandwich. This will create a crunchy cheddar crust on each slice.

**4/** Heat the pan over medium heat for 1 minute before cooking the sandwiches, two at a time, for 3–4 minutes on each side. Serve once you have a golden and toasted cheddar crust.

# Taleggio, mozzarella, prosciutto, olive ± basil flatbreads.

**This is my go-to midweek sandwich – so easy, but delicious. Chuck the dough ingredients into a mixer for a few minutes and leave to rest for 30 minutes.**

### Pro tip
You can use any fillings you want; my combo here is just a suggestion (a delicious one, though). Give this a try and it will become a favourite. I make it once a week with whatever fillings I have in my refrigerator.

### Makes
4

### Prep time
40 minutes (plus standing)

### Toasting method
Pan

### Bread
4 home-made flatbreads (as in recipe below)

*250 g (9 oz/1⅔ cups) 00 flour, plus extra for dusting*
*20 g (¾ oz) unsalted butter, softened*
*1 tablespoon plain yoghurt*
*125 ml (4 fl oz/½ cup) full-cream (whole) milk*
*1 teaspoon salt flakes*
*160 g (5½ oz) taleggio, sliced*
*100 g (3½ oz) prosciutto*
*4 Roasted tomatoes (page 14), halved*
*60 g (2 oz) Ligurian olives, pitted and sliced*
*160 g (5½ oz) mozzarella, torn*
*fresh basil leaves*
*freshly ground black pepper*

**1/** Place the flour, butter, yoghurt, milk and salt in a bowl and knead with your hands to form a dough. Turn the dough out onto a lightly floured work surface and knead for 4 minutes until you have a smooth and stretchy dough. Form the dough into a ball and wrap it in plastic wrap. Rest the dough at room temperature for 30 minutes.

**2/** Cut the dough into four even pieces. On a lightly floured work surface, roll out each piece of dough into a 20 cm (8 in) round. Stack the flatbread rounds in between pieces of lightly floured baking paper to stop them sticking to the bench.

**3/** Heat a large non-stick frying pan over medium heat and cook one flatbread at a time. Cook for 1 minute or until the surface of the flatbread starts to bubble and expand. Flip the bread over and add a quarter of the sliced taleggio to one half of the bread. To the same half add some prosciutto, two tomato halves, some sliced olives and basil leaves before topping with mozzarella and pepper. Fold the empty side of the flatbread over the mozzarella and flip the flatbread over. Cook for a couple of minutes and flip again if needed to ensure the cheese has melted. Reserve, cover with a cloth and keep warm. Cook the remaining flatbreads and serve immediately with more fresh basil leaves and a grinding of pepper.

# End.

(SWEET THINGS)

# Dark chocolate, olive oil ± Murray River salt flakes.

This is another Spanish-inspired combination and it is sensational. It's quick and never fails to deliver. When you only have a few ingredients, they all need to count. Use the best bread, olive oil, salt and chocolate that you can afford.

### Pro tips
Salt really balances the sweetness and enhances the flavour of the chocolate. I use Barry Callebaut Dark 67% Madagascan chocolate melts (buttons).

### Makes
4

### Prep time
10 minutes

### Toasting method
Toasted sandwich press

### Bread
8 thin slices white sandwich loaf

*80 ml (2½ fl oz/⅓ cup) Arbequina olive oil (see page 159)*
*160 g (5½ oz) dark chocolate melts (buttons) – minimum 65% cocoa solids*
*Murray River salt flakes*

**1/** Liberally drizzle olive oil on all the bread slices and evenly add chocolate melts to four of them. Sprinkle salt flakes on the chocolate and top with the remaining slices of bread. Push down and again drizzle with olive oil.

**2/** Heat a toasted sandwich press and cook the sandwiches for 4–5 minutes until golden and toasted. Remove from the press and leave to sit for 1 minute. Drizzle with oil and additional salt and serve.

# Explosive raspberry melt.

 WTF???

**BOOM! This should come with a warning. Eat this sandwich outside…it could go off! This is one of my signature flavours that I couldn't resist turning into a melt. The popping candy makes it explosive.**

## Pro tips
Brioche is the way to go here, and chocolate-coated popping candy can be found online. I use Barry Callebaut milk chocolate melts (buttons) for this one, but any good-quality milk chocolate will do. Chop it into small pieces if it comes in a block.

**Makes**
**4**

**Prep time**
**45 minutes (plus standing)**

**Toasting method**
**Grill (broiler)**

**Bread**
**8 slices brioche loaf**

80 g (2¾ oz) unsalted butter
1 tablespoon icing
    (confectioners') sugar
125 g (4½ oz/1 cup) raspberries
80 g (2¾ oz) chocolate-coated
    popping candy

*Chocolate ganache*
260 g (9 oz) good-quality milk
    chocolate melts (buttons)
80 g (2¾ oz) unsalted butter,
    softened
250 ml (8½ fl oz/1 cup)
    thickened (whipping) cream

*Marshmallow*
5 gold-strength gelatine leaves
2 egg whites
200 g (7 oz) caster (superfine)
    sugar
1 teaspoon liquid glucose
4 tablespoons freeze-dried
    raspberry powder

**1/** For the chocolate ganache, put the chocolate and butter in a tall plastic jug.

**2/** Put the cream in a saucepan over medium heat and bring to the boil. Pour it into the jug with the the chocolate and butter. Leave to sit for 20 seconds before blending to a smooth and shiny cream, using a hand-held blender. Transfer the mixture to a clean plastic container and rest some plastic wrap on the surface so a skin doesn't form. Leave at room temperature for a few hours to harden.

**3/** For the marshmallow, soak the gelatine in cold water for 2 minutes to soften. Squeeze to remove the excess water and discard the water.

**4/** Place the egg whites in the clean bowl of a freestanding electric mixer fitted with the whisk attachment, and start to whisk on low speed.

**5/** Combine 75 ml (2½ fl oz) water, the caster sugar and glucose in a small saucepan over medium heat. Stir gently to dissolve the sugar and bring the syrup to the boil. Turn the mixer with the egg whites to medium speed.

**6/** Cook the syrup to 125°C (257°F), using a digital or sugar thermometer to check the temperature. Slowly pour the syrup into the whisking egg whites – pour in a constant stream down one side of the bowl to avoid the whisk. Once all the syrup has been added, turn the machine to high speed.

**7/** Add the soaked gelatine to the hot saucepan. The residual heat will melt the gelatine, which can then be added to the mixing bowl once it is fluid. Whisk well until the mixture starts to cool and thicken and then add 3 tablespoons of the freeze-dried raspberry powder and again mix to combine. Transfer the marshmallow mixture to a piping (icing) bag fitted with a medium-sized plain nozzle.

**8/** Assemble the sandwiches when the ganache is thick and set. Preheat a grill (broiler) to hot. Mix the butter with the icing sugar and use a spoon to mix well. Butter one side of each of the eight slices of brioche with the sweetened butter and toast these sides under the grill. Remove from the grill and turn the brioche slices over to build the sandwiches on the uncooked side.

**9/** Liberally spread the chocolate ganache on each slice with a small palette knife, pushing it to the edges of the brioche. Add the whole fresh raspberries and pipe bulbs of marshmallow to completely cover the surface of the raspberries and chocolate cream. Top the sandwiches with the remaining brioche slices, butter side up, and gently press down. Use a sharp knife to cut the sandwiches into triangles and scatter with the popping candy.

# Chocolate ± caramel spread w̲ hazelnuts.

Is there a better combo than chocolate and hazelnut? This is a great recipe for a quick, rich chocolate spread.

## Pro tips
You could use a sourdough bread here or even a seeded sourdough. I am sticking to my old-school white sandwich, which was what I used for my Nutella sandwiches after school all those years ago. Again I am using Barry Callebaut dark chocolate melts (buttons). You could use these or any other good-quality chocolate. If it comes in a block, then chop it into small pieces with a knife.

## Makes
4

## Prep time
45 minutes (plus cooling)

## Toasting method
Toasted sandwich press

## Bread
8 slices white sandwich loaf

140 g (5 oz) caster (superfine) sugar
25 g (1 oz) jam-setting sugar
400 ml (13½ fl oz) thickened (whipping) cream
1 tablespoon liquid glucose
salt flakes
75 g (2¾ oz) dark chocolate, chopped
80 g (2¾ oz) hazelnuts, skinned, toasted and roughly chopped
softened butter, for spreading

**1/** Place a large heavy-based saucepan over medium heat and allow the pan to get hot for 1 minute. Gradually add the caster sugar, stirring constantly with a heat-resistant spatula or wooden spoon, until all the sugar has been incorporated and you have a dark amber caramel.

**2/** Put the jam-setting sugar, cream, glucose and a pinch of salt flakes in a separate saucepan over medium heat and bring to the boil. Remove the pan from the heat and add this mixture to the hot caramel – be extremely careful as the mixture will bubble and spit and the steam is dangerously hot. Mix well, then reduce the heat to low, return the pan to the stove top and cook for around 10 minutes until the volume is reduced by half.

**3/** Put the chocolate in a jug or bowl. Pour half the hot caramel mixture onto the chocolate and use a hand-held blender to process the mixture until smooth, before adding the rest of the caramel. Blend again until smooth. Pour into hot sterilised jam jars and seal, or pour into a container and store in the refrigerator. Once set, the spread can be used straight away.

**4/** Liberally spread the chocolate and caramel mixture on eight slices of bread. Add chopped hazelnuts and salt flakes to four of the slices. Sandwich the four hazelnut slices together with the four other slices. Heat a toasted sandwich press, brush the outsides of each sandwich with softened butter and cook until golden brown.

# Dark chocolate, Roquefort ± vanilla cherries.

Blue cheese and cherries work very well together but, with a good-quality dark chocolate, these crisp breads will be a finish to a meal that everyone will remember.

### Pro tips
Make a big batch of the Vanilla cherries as they are sensational and work well as a quick dessert with ice cream.
I prefer Roquefort for this recipe, but gorgonzola or Stilton work just as well.

### Makes
**12 toasts for 4 people**

### Prep time
**10 minutes**

### Toasting method
**Grill (broiler)**

### Bread
**1 baguette, cut diagonally into twelve 1 cm (½ in) thick slices**

*60 ml (2 fl oz/¼ cup) light olive oil*
*100 g (3½ oz) block of good-quality, single origin dark chocolate (65% cocoa solids)*
*120 g (4½ oz) Roquefort*
*125 g (4½ oz) Vanilla cherries (page 24)*

**1/** Preheat a grill (broiler) to hot. Drizzle the olive oil over the bread slices and place them on a baking tray lined with baking paper. Toast the slices well on both sides under the grill.

**2/** Grate the chocolate evenly over one side of the slices. Crumble around 10 g (¼ oz) of Roquefort on top of each slice with your fingers, top with the vanilla cherries and serve.

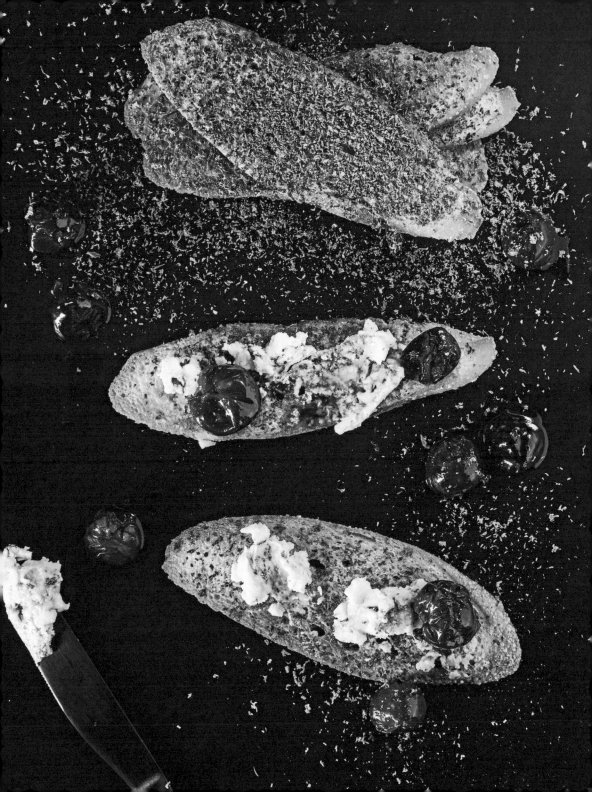

# White chocolate ±
# strawberry toast.

**Simply put, this open toast is silky, smooth, sweet and very binge-worthy. The white chocolate cream is easy to make and is the perfect foil to the concentrated flavour of the strawberries.**

## Pro tips
The strawberries take on a more intense flavour and the jammy syrup that comes out of them is absolutely delicious. Brioche is again the go here and the slices should ideally be bar-marked on a barbecue or in a chargrill pan before serving.

## Makes
4

## Prep time
**40 minutes (plus cooling)**

## Toasting method
**Barbecue/chargrill pan and oven**

## Bread
**4 slices brioche loaf**

500 g (1 lb 2 oz) strawberries, hulled and halved
2 tablespoons caster (superfine) sugar
250 g (9 oz) White chocolate cream (page 23)

**1/** Preheat the oven to 180°C (350°F). Place the strawberries in a non-stick baking tin. Sprinkle the sugar over the strawberries and place the tin in the oven. Cook for 25 minutes, then remove the strawberries from the oven. Leave the strawberries to cool in the tin.

**2/** Toast the brioche slices on a barbecue or in a chargrill pan to bar-mark the bread. Set aside to cool.

**3/** Place the toast on serving plates and spoon 3 tablespoons of white chocolate cream onto the toast. Add the warm roasted strawberries and serve.

# Dark chocolate ± orange marshmallow waffle.

The marshmallow is the toasted part of this, and who can resist toasted marshmallow! Chocolate and orange is a classic combo and, although simple, this creation feels like you are in a fancy restaurant.

## Pro tips
I have found a bakery that makes amazing, sweet and fluffy, but slightly crunchy, waffles. They are the perfect sweet bed for the chocolate cream, orange syrup and marshmallow here. You could also use store-bought waffles if you wish – just give them 10 seconds in a microwave to freshen them up before serving. I am using a posh chocolate here. It's a high cocoa content, single-origin dark chocolate, which I love. You can use a good-quality dark chocolate if you can't find this one.

**Makes**
4

**Prep time**
40 minutes (plus standing)

**Toasting method**
Pan

**Bread**
4 thick waffles

*Candied orange slices*
    *(page 25)*
*1 tablespoon icing*
    *(confectioners') sugar*
    *for dusting*

*Chocolate and orange ganache*
*225 g (8 oz) Barry Callebaut*
    *Dark 67% Madagascan*
    *chocolate melts (buttons)*
*90 g (3 oz) unsalted butter,*
    *softened*
*½ orange (for zesting)*
*250 ml (8½ fl oz/1 cup)*
    *thickened (whipping) cream*

*Marshmallow*
*5 gold-strength gelatine leaves*
*2 egg whites*
*200 g (7 oz) caster (superfine)*
    *sugar*
*1 teaspoon liquid glucose*
*½ orange (for zesting)*

**1/** For the chocolate and orange ganache, put the chocolate and butter in a tall plastic jug.

**2/** Grate the orange zest into a saucepan and add the cream. Bring to the boil over medium heat, then pour the mixture over the chocolate and butter. Leave to sit for 20 seconds before blending to a smooth and shiny cream, using a hand-held blender. Transfer the mixture to a clean plastic container and rest some plastic wrap on the surface so a skin doesn't form. Leave at room temperature for a few hours to harden.

**3/** For the marshmallow, soak the gelatine in cold water for 2 minutes to soften. Squeeze to remove the excess water and discard the water. Place the egg whites in the clean bowl of a freestanding electric mixer fitted with the whisk attachment, and start to whisk on low speed.

**4/** Place 75 ml (2½ fl oz) water, the caster sugar and glucose in a small saucepan over medium heat and stir gently to dissolve the sugar and bring the syrup to the boil.

**5/** Turn the mixer with the egg whites to medium speed. Cook the syrup to 125°C (257°F), using a digital or sugar thermometer to check the temperature. Slowly pour the syrup into the whisking egg whites – pour it in a constant stream down one side of the bowl to avoid the whisk. Once all the syrup has been added, turn the machine to high speed.

**6/** Add the soaked gelatine to the hot saucepan. The residual heat will melt the gelatine, which can be added to the mixing bowl once it is fluid. Whisk well until the mixture starts to cool and thicken, then grate in the orange zest.

**7/** Add a spoonful of the ganache to the waffles, then spoon over some candied orange slices in syrup. Top with a large dollop of orange marshmallow and lightly toast the marshmallow with a blowtorch or under a hot grill (broiler). Dust with icing sugar and serve.

# Olive oil toast w̲ white chocolate, caviar ± Champagne.

FANCY...

A little bit posh, these melts are for VIPs only. The salty caviar works brilliantly with the crunchy toast and sweet white chocolate. All washed down with bubbly, this celebration will go down in history.

**Pro tip**
Omit the jelly if it's too much hassle – these melts work just as well with only the white chocolate and caviar. Make sure the Champagne goes to good use, though – cheers!

**Makes**
4

**Prep time**
45 minutes (plus chilling)

**Toasting method**
Grill (broiler)

**Bread**
1 baguette, sliced into twelve 1 cm (½ in) thick slices, cut diagonally

60 ml (2 fl oz/¼ cup) extra-virgin olive oil
80 g (2¾ oz) good-quality block white chocolate
30 g (1 oz) black caviar

*Champagne jelly*
2 gold-strength gelatine leaves
225 ml (7½ fl oz) Champagne
25 g (1 oz) caster (superfine) sugar

**1/** For the Champagne jelly, soak the gelatine in cold water. Put half the Champagne and the sugar in a small saucepan over medium heat. Stir the liquid to dissolve the sugar, then remove the pan from the heat. Drain the gelatine, squeeze out the excess water and discard the water. Stir the gelatine into the hot sugar syrup to melt it. Add the remaining Champagne and stir again to mix well. Strain the mixture through a small sieve into a small plastic container and store the jelly in the refrigerator for a couple of hours before serving.

**2/** Preheat a grill (broiler) to hot. Drizzle the olive oil over the bread slices and place them on a baking tray lined with baking paper. Toast the slices well on both sides under the grill and remove. Liberally grate the white chocolate over the warm slices and allow the heat to melt the chocolate.

**3/** Place the slices on a serving plate. Take the jelly out of the refrigerator and, using a warmed teaspoon, 'cut' out small scoops of jelly and place them just off-centre on the slices of toast. Use a non-metallic spoon to scoop a small teaspoon of caviar onto each slice next to the jelly and serve immediately.

# Apple ± blackberry jaffle w̲ custard.

Apple and blackberry has always been a favourite combination for me. I used to love a good apple and blackberry crumble when I was young, and still do. No matter what your age, crumble should always come with custard.

## Pro tips
This recipe features a revolutionary cooking technique, where the apples are cooked in the microwave, which ensures all the moisture is retained and the fruit becomes translucent, intensifies in flavour but does not go to mush. The sweetened spiced sugar ensures a crispy jaffle exterior.

## Makes
4

## Prep time
40 minutes

## Toasting method
Jaffle maker

## Bread
8 slices white sandwich loaf

8 pink lady (or other sweet pink) apples (about 800 g/ 1 lb 12 oz)
1 vanilla bean, seeds scraped
finely grated zest and juice of 1 lemon
125 g (4½ oz) caster (superfine) sugar
80 g (2¾ oz) unsalted butter, softened
½ teaspoon cinnamon
1 tablespoon raw (demerara) sugar
16 fresh blackberries, or you can use frozen
icing (confectioners') sugar for dusting
Vanilla custard (page 23), to serve

1/ Peel the apples, cut them into quarters and remove the core. Cut each quarter into four pieces and place the apple, with the vanilla seeds and pod, lemon juice and zest and the sugar, in a glass, microwave-proof dish with a lid that allows the steam to escape. Cook in the microwave on High (100%) for 5 minutes, then stir to ensure even cooking. Repeat this process until the apples are cooked, about 15–25 minutes. The apples are ready when the pieces are whole but soft, translucent but not puréed. Leave them to cool completely before making the sandwiches. Discard the vanilla pod.

2/ Mix the butter with the cinnamon and raw sugar using a spoon. Heat a jaffle maker. Butter one side of each slice of bread with the flavoured butter. Assemble the four sandwiches by making them one at a time directly inside the jaffle maker. Place two or three heaped tablespoons of cooled apple filling in the centre of the non-buttered side of bread and push four blackberries in per sandwich. Close the sandwich with the remaining slices of bread, butter side up. Cook the jaffles for 4 minutes or until golden-brown and sealed. Remove and cut in half and dust with icing sugar before serving with the cold custard.

# Chocolate ± hazelnut melt w̲ orange blossom.

My friend, baker Michael James from Tivoli Road Bakery, seriously makes the best croissants. They are delicious and I couldn't resist using one (or four) for this decadent melts. It's my version of those almond croissants you can find in great bakeries like Michael's.

## Pro tips

The hazelnut mix is a sort of take on the classic almond frangipane, and the orange blossom water adds a new dimension. Only toast the croissants lightly to get flowing chocolate that's not overcooked.

## Makes

4

## Prep time

30 minutes

## Toasting method

Toasted sandwich press and oven

## Bread

4 croissants, sliced in half

80 g (2¾ oz) unsalted butter, softened
pinch of salt flakes
1 vanilla bean, seeds scraped
80 g (2¾ oz) icing (confectioners') sugar
80 g (2¾ oz/¾ cup) ground hazelnuts
1 egg
1 tablespoon orange blossom water
100 g (3½ oz) thin block of good-quality dark chocolate, broken into squares
40 g (1½ oz/¼ cup) hazelnuts, shelled, toasted and coarsely chopped

**1/** Place the butter, salt, scraped vanilla seeds and icing sugar in the bowl of a freestanding electric mixer fitted with the paddle attachment. Mix the ingredients on low speed for 5 minutes before scraping the inside of the bowl down with a spatula to ensure the butter is evenly distributed. Add the ground hazelnuts and mix again on low speed for 5 minutes. Scrape the bowl down again and mix for a further minute before adding the egg. Mix for a couple of minutes, then add the orange blossom water and again mix to combine.

**2/** Preheat the oven to 180°C (350°F). Place a quarter of the squares of chocolate on each croissant. Use a palette knife to spread the hazelnut cream evenly over the chocolate, spreading right to the edges of the croissant. Close the croissants.

**3/** Heat a sandwich press and cook the croissants for 3–4 minutes until you have a crispy exterior.

**4/** Place the croissants on a baking tray, then transfer them to the oven and bake for 5 minutes. Remove from the oven, sprinkle the sliced hazelnuts onto each croissant and serve immediately.

# Caramelised peach <u>w</u> amaretto brioche toast ± vanilla ice cream.

When peaches are in season they are to be savoured and celebrated. This is a really fabulous melt that champions the peach – and anything with ice cream is immediately improved, even a melt.

**Pro tip**
Use ripe peaches to make it easier to get the skin off.

**Makes**
4

**Prep time**
50 minutes (plus chilling)

**Toasting method**
Pan

**Bread**
four 5 × 2 cm (2 × 1 in) slices brioche loaf, crusts removed and trimmed to uniform-sized squares or rectangles

120 g (4½ oz) Nut crumble mix (page 25)
300 ml (10 fl oz) full-cream (whole) milk
50 ml (1¾ fl oz) amaretto liqueur
4 eggs, lightly beaten
pinch of salt flakes
120 g (4½ oz) icing (confectioners') sugar
2 loose-stone peaches
iced water
caster (superfine) sugar for sprinkling
60 g (2 oz) unsalted butter, softened
4 scoops vanilla ice cream, to serve

**1/** Put the brioche slices in a sealed container and place them in the refrigerator for 1 hour to dry out and harden up (this will help with soaking).

**2/** Preheat the oven to 165°C (330°F). Put the raw nut crumble mix on a baking tray lined with baking paper. Bake in the oven for 12–15 minutes until golden brown. Set aside.

**3/** Combine the milk, amaretto liqueur, eggs, salt and 40 g (1½ oz) of the icing sugar. Mix together well, then strain through a sieve into a shallow dish. Soak the brioche slices for 15 minutes before flipping each slice and soaking for a further 15 minutes to get maximum coverage. Remove each slice from the dish and place on a wire rack over a tray to catch the drips. Leave for 10 minutes to drain.

**4/** Use a sharp paring knife to cut a cross on the bottom of the two peaches.

**5/** Bring a saucepan of water to the boil over medium heat. Plunge the peaches into the boiling water and remove them with a slotted spoon after 25 seconds. Refresh the peaches in iced water for 2 minutes before peeling away the skins using a paring knife. Cut the peaches in half and discard the stone. Sprinkle the peaches with caster sugar and caramelise them with a blowtorch or under a hot grill (broiler).

**6/** Heat the softened butter in a non-stick frying pan over medium heat until just melted. Dust each drained slice of brioche with the remaining icing sugar. Add the slices of brioche to the pan and cook them for a couple of minutes until golden brown and caramelised. Flip each slice and cook until golden and caramelised on the other side.

**7/** Remove the brioche slices from the pan and place them in four serving bowls. Add the caramelised fruit and cooked nut crumble, and serve with vanilla ice cream.

# Lamington pain perdu – ooooh, look at you!

Lamingtons have become a big part of my life – admittedly too big. However, these simply constructed, but difficult-to-master, classics are something to celebrate.

## Pro tips

Get as much jam as poss into these, as it is key. We are using a variation on a classic French toast method here again, and brioche is always the best option bread-wise for this. If you are a little bit better than everyone else, then you can call this a pain perdu – but just check yo-self. This is just a sandwich book after all. Try to use a chocolate block instead of melts (buttons) as you need to grate some of it at the end.

## Makes
4

## Prep time
45 minutes (plus chilling)

## Toasting method
Pan

## Bread
four 5 cm (2 in) slices brioche loaf, crusts removed and trimmed to 5 cm (2 in) cubes

100 g (3½ oz) dark chocolate, plus extra for grating
150 ml (5 fl oz) full-cream (whole) milk
2 eggs, lightly beaten
pinch of salt flakes
100 g (3½ oz) icing (confectioners') sugar
50 g (1¾ oz) butter, softened
50 g (1¾ oz) raspberry jam
50 g (1¾ oz) fresh coconut
80 ml (2½ fl oz/⅓ cup) thickened (whipping) cream, to serve
30 g (2 oz/¼ cup) fresh raspberries, to serve

**1/** Put the brioche cubes in a sealed container and place them in the refrigerator for 1 hour to dry out and harden up (this will help with soaking). Put the chocolate in a bowl.

**2/** Put the milk in a saucepan over medium heat and bring to the boil. Remove from the heat. Melt half the chocolate and reserve the remaining chocolate for the end. Pour the scalded milk over the melted chocolate and stir to combine, then add the eggs, salt and 20 g (¾ oz) of the icing sugar. Mix well together with a whisk or fork and then strain through a sieve into a shallow dish.

**3/** Place the brioche cubes in the dish to soak. Soak the cubes for 15 minutes and then flip them after 15 minutes to get maximum coverage. Remove the brioche cubes from the dish and place them on a wire rack over a tray to catch the drips. Leave for 10 minutes to drain.

**4/** Heat the softened butter in a non-stick frying pan over medium heat until just melted. Dust each drained cube of brioche with the remaining icing sugar. Add the cubes of brioche to the pan and cook them for a couple of minutes on each side until golden brown and caramelised. Flip each cube and cook until golden and caramelised on the other side.

**5/** Remove the brioche cubes from the pan and place them in a dish. Cut each cube in half and spoon some raspberry jam into the centre of each, then top off with the lid. Grate dark chocolate over the lamingtons while they are still warm, and finish by grating the coconut over, using a microplane. Serve with cream and fresh raspberries.

# Roast balsamic strawberry, ricotta, mascarpone ± chocolate.

**A beautiful balance of sweet strawberries, creamy mascarpone, acidic vinegar and ricotta. Toast never tasted so decadent.**

## Pro tips
There's a lot going on here but it all works together well. The microplane-grated chocolate technique is great to add not too much chocolate to a dish. Both white and dark are used here and, again, try to buy a good-quality chocolate.

## Makes
4

## Prep time
**40 minutes (plus cooling)**

## Toasting method
**Toaster or grill (broiler)**

## Bread
**4 slices sourdough loaf**

40 g (1½ oz) good-quality dark chocolate
200 g (7 oz) ricotta
100 ml (3½ fl oz) thickened (whipping) cream
100 g (3½ oz) mascarpone
60 g (2 oz) good-quality white chocolate, finely grated, plus extra to serve

_Roasted strawberries_
500 g (1 lb 2 oz) strawberries, hulled and halved
2 tablespoons caster (superfine) sugar
75 ml (2½ fl oz) aged balsamic vinegar (ideally from Modena)

**1/** For the roasted strawberries, preheat the oven to 180°C (350°F). Put the strawberries in a non-stick baking tin. Sprinkle the sugar over, then the balsamic vinegar. Place the tray in the oven and cook the strawberries for 25 minutes. Remove from the oven and leave the strawberries to cool in the tin.

**2/** Toast the sourdough bread in a toaster or under a grill (broiler) and remove from the heat. Place the slices on a baking tray lined with baking paper. While the toast is still warm, finely grate the dark chocolate onto each slice using a microplane.

**3/** Place the ricotta and cream in a bowl and stir with a silicone spatula to combine them. Use a small hand-held whisk to thicken the cream to soft peaks. Fold in the mascarpone and grated white chocolate.

**4/** Spread or spoon the cream onto each piece of toast and transfer the toast to individual plates. Top with the cooled strawberries and the excess cooking juices, then grate over some white chocolate and serve.

# Peanut butter, raspberry ± milk chocolate melt.

Imagine a melt that has peanut butter and raspberries, which you could dip in milk chocolate as you pleased. Well, look no further...

## Pro tips

Salty peanut butter works really well with the tart raspberries. Brioche is key and milk chocolate makes the whole world a better place. Use smooth or crunchy peanut butter, whatever your preference.

## Makes
4

## Prep time
15 minutes

## Toasting method
Pan

## Bread
8 slices brioche loaf

*120 g (4½ oz) peanut butter*
*4 tablespoons raspberry jam*
*16 raspberries, halved*
*80 g (2¾ oz) unsalted butter, softened*
*600 g (1 lb 5 oz) Callebaut Origin Java 32% milk chocolate melts (buttons), melted, for dipping*

**1/** Liberally spread peanut butter evenly onto four slices of the brioche. Spread the raspberry jam on the remaining slices and evenly distribute the halved raspberries on top. Sandwich the peanut butter and raspberry slices together. Make four sandwiches in total and butter the outside of each.

**2/** Heat a large non-stick frying pan over medium heat. Cook the sandwiches for 4 minutes on each side to obtain a golden exterior. Remove the sandwiches from the heat and allow them to cool before cutting them into strips, or in half lengthways. Serve with the melted milk chocolate for dipping.

CHOCOLATE SOLDIERS

# Coffee-infused French toast <u>w</u> banana, nut crumble ± yoghurt.

One of my signature flavour combos is coffee, banana and passionfruit – absolutely delish. This is another French toast–style dish with the soaking custard flavoured with coffee. This one is fantastic as breakfast.

### Pro tip
You could use fresh coffee beans to infuse if you don't have a pod machine at home, or even instant coffee will work fine.

### Makes
4

### Prep time
50 minutes (plus chilling and standing)

### Toasting method
Pan and oven

### Bread
four 3 cm (1¼ in) slices brioche loaf, crusts removed and trimmed to equal-sized squares or rectangles

300 ml (10 fl oz) full-cream (whole) milk
2 Nespresso coffee pods
4 eggs, lightly beaten
pinch of salt flakes
120 g (4½ oz) icing (confectioners') sugar
60 g (2 oz) unsalted butter, softened
2 bananas, sliced
140 g (5 oz) Nut crumble mix (page 25)
4 tablespoons Greek-style yoghurt
seeds from 2 passionfruit

**1/** Put the brioche slices in a sealed container and place them in the refrigerator for 1 hour to dry out and harden up (this will help with soaking).

**2/** Use a sharp knife to cut open the foil top of the two coffee pods and pour the ground coffee into a small saucepan with the milk. Bring the coffee milk to the boil and set aside for ten minutes to infuse. Put the eggs, salt and 40 g (1½ oz) of the icing sugar in a bowl. Pour the milk and coffee mixture into the bowl and whisk well to combine. Strain through a sieve into a shallow dish.

**3/** Place the brioche slices in the dish to soak. Soak the slices for 15 minutes and then flip them after 15 minutes to get maximum coverage. Remove each slice from the dish and place on a wire rack over a tray to catch the drips. Leave for 10 minutes to drain.

**4/** Preheat the oven to 180°C (350°F).

**5/** Heat the softened butter in a non-stick frying pan over medium heat until just melted. Dust each drained slice of brioche with the remaining icing sugar. Add the slices of brioche to the pan and cook them for a couple of minutes until golden brown and caramelised. Flip each slice and cook until golden and caramelised on the other side.

**6/** Remove the brioche slices from the pan and transfer to a baking tray lined with baking paper. Place the banana slices on each slice of toast and top with the nut crumble mix. Bake in the oven for 15 minutes until the crumble is cooked to golden brown. Remove from the oven and serve with the yoghurt and fresh passionfruit seeds.

# Cherry blossom ±
# miso French toast.

The cherry blossom season in Japan is extremely important and significant. Cherry blossom has a unique flavour that resembles almonds, and it goes well with desserts as well as savoury dishes.

### Pro tip
Sakura cherry blossom paste can be found online or in Asian or Japanese food stores. It is highly concentrated so you don't need much. If you can't find it, you could use some of the liquid from the Vanilla cherries instead.

### Makes
4

### Prep time
**30 minutes (plus chilling and standing)**

### Toasting method
**Pan**

### Bread
**four 5 cm (2 in) thick slices brioche loaf, crusts removed and trimmed to 5 cm (2 in) cubes**

300 ml (10½ fl oz) full-cream (whole) milk
30 g (1 oz) Sakura cherry blossom paste
4 eggs, lightly beaten
120 g (4½ oz) icing (confectioners') sugar
250 g (9 oz) Caramel cream (page 24)
25 g (1 oz) white miso paste
60 g (2 oz) unsalted butter, softened
100 g (3½ oz) Vanilla cherries (page 24)
vanilla ice cream, to serve

**1/** Put the brioche cubes in a sealed container and place them in the refrigerator for a few hours to dry out and harden up (this will help with soaking).

**2/** Combine the milk, cherry blossom paste, eggs and 40 g (1½ oz/⅓ cup) of the icing sugar. Mix well together, then strain through a sieve into a shallow dish.

**3/** Remove the brioche from the refrigerator and place the cubes in the dish to soak. Store in the refrigerator for a minimum of 1 hour. Flip each cube after 15 minutes or so to get maximum coverage.

**4/** Remove each cube from the dish and place on a wire rack over a tray to catch the drips. Leave for 20 minutes to drain.

**5/** Use a spatula to mix the caramel cream evenly with the miso paste. Transfer to a piping (icing) bag fitted with a small plain nozzle.

**6/** Heat the softened butter in a non-stick frying pan over medium heat until just melted. Dust each drained cube of brioche with the remaining icing sugar. Add the brioche cubes to the pan and cook them for a couple of minutes until golden brown and caramelised. Flip each cube and cook until golden and caramelised on the other side.

**7/** Remove from the pan and place the brioche cubes in four serving bowls. Top with the vanilla cherries and their syrup and pipe small bulbs of the miso caramel around it. Serve with vanilla ice cream.

# White chocolate, raspberry, almond, rose ± vanilla.

White chocolate. Almond. Raspberry. Rose. Back up the truck – I'm there! Delicate and delicious, this coming together of great flavours makes for a beautiful toast dish. You'll be coming back to this again and again.

**Pro tips**

I've used delicious Barry Callebaut chocolate melts (buttons) here, but any good-quality white chocolate will do. Omit the rosewater if you're not keen.

**Makes**
4

**Prep time**
1 hour

**Toasting method**
Toaster and oven

**Bread**
four 2 cm (¾ in) thick slices brioche loaf

60 g (2 oz) raspberry jam
160 g (5½ oz) unsalted butter, softened
pinch of salt flakes
2 vanilla beans, seeds scraped
160 g (5½ oz) icing (confectioners') sugar, plus extra for dusting
160 g (5½ oz) ground almonds
2 eggs
2 tablespoons rosewater
80 g (2¾ oz) white chocolate melts (buttons)
125 g (4½ oz/1 cup) raspberries, halved

**1/** Lightly toast the brioche slices on both sides using a toaster and spread the jam evenly on one side of each slice.

**2/** Place the butter, salt, scraped vanilla seeds and icing sugar in the bowl of a freestanding electric mixer fitted with the paddle attachment. Mix the ingredients together on low speed for 5 minutes before scraping the inside of the bowl down with a spatula to ensure the butter is evenly distributed. Add the ground almonds and mix again on low speed for 5 minutes. Scrape the bowl down again and mix for a further minute before adding the eggs. Mix for a couple of minutes, then add the rosewater and mix to combine. Transfer to a piping (icing) bag fitted with a plain nozzle.

**3/** Preheat the oven to 180°C (350°F).

**4/** Sprinkle the chocolate melts onto the jam. Pipe the almond cream evenly on top, covering the chocolate melts. Place the four completed slices of bread on a baking tray lined with baking paper and chill in the refrigerator for 10 minutes.

**5/** Remove the bread from the refrigerator and add the halved raspberries, pushing them into the almond cream. Bake the slices in the oven for 30 minutes until golden brown. Remove from the oven and dust with icing sugar before serving immediately.

# Cheese matters.

All chefs will tell you they are only as good as their ingredients, and I always try to use the best I can afford. My friend and cheese expert Anthony Femia, from Maker & Monger at Prahran Market in Melbourne, supplied the cheeses in this book – I asked him for a few notes on each cheese to help you get the most out of your melts. If you are ever in Melbourne do check him out, or you can visit his website makerandmonger.com.au.

### Montgomery cheddar
**Somerset, England**

The King of cloth-bound cheddars, this cheese has the perfect melting texture and exhibits rich beef broth flavours with grassy undernotes. You should always match this cheese with equally rich ingredients for the ultimate Sunday brunch melt.

### Bay of Fires cloth-bound cheddar
**Bay of Fires Cheese, Tasmania**

A 13th-generation cheesemaker, Englishman Ian Fowlers draws on traditional methods used by his family to produce his cloth-bound cheddar at St Helens on the east coast of Tasmania. He makes and matures his cheddars in repurposed shipping containers.

### Asiago
**Veneto, Italy**

There are two different types of Asiago on the market. The young Pressato is pliable, with soft notes of sweetness and acid, and has a great pH for melting, resulting in a very stringy pull. The matured Asiago is aged like a parmesan with deeper flavours and a denser texture.

### Gouda
**Holland**

Aged gouda has an incredibly rich and lingering caramel flavour with crunchy calcium crystals adding to the sensory delight of this cheese. Be careful though, as gouda separates during melting, with the fats and proteins splitting and causing a clear liquid residue that runs off the plate.

### Emmental
**France and Switzerland**

Emmental is one of the best melting cheeses and the main ingredient of delicious fondue. Its pH level gives it the perfect melting point, resulting in a molten liquid that is stringy and holds its shape at the same time.

### Bulgarian feta

A softer style of feta than its Greek counterpart, it has a slightly sweet and creamy flavour with a citrus tang.

### Gorgonzola piccante
**Lombardy, Italy**

An aged cow's milk blue cheese from the north of Italy with a slight crumbly texture and prominent blue spice on the palate. It has a low melting point due to its high moisture content, so don't overcook it.

### Parmigiano Reggiano
**Emilia-Romagna, Italy**

Look for Reggiano aged 18 months or less for an incredibly sweet and rich flavour. Reggiano will always slightly separate when melted, with the fats becoming a clear liquid. Reggiano always brings out the best in its paired ingredients, so get ready for a delicious treat when melting this cheese.

### Gruyère
**Fribourg, Switzerland**

Another of the staple melting cheeses, this alpine cheese melts to a perfect texture with incredible stringiness when pulled. Rich and nutty flavours abounding, this is perfect for your melts.

### Raclette
**Australia, Switzerland and France**

Make sure you use the rind of raclette when grilling, as this washed-rind, semi-hard cheese exhibits all its incredible flavours in its rind. Smelly, yet savoury, raclette has a beautiful melting texture and adds another dimension to your toasted cheese sandwich.

### Fontina Val d'Aosta
**Val d'Aosta, Italy**

Italy's answer to raclette, this washed-rind alpine cheese has an incredibly savoury flavour with a lingering sharpness. A perfect uniform melting texture gives way to a robust aroma and flavour when this cheese is grilled with its rind.

### Comté
**Franche-Comté, France**

The most popular cheese in France and rightly so! Comté can be eaten any time of the day. It exhibits a beautiful floral aroma with distinct flavours reminiscent of cashew nuts and honey. This French gruyère is the benchmark for all melting cheeses with its perfect melting texture and flavour release.

### Taleggio
**Lombardy, Italy**

An Italian washed-rind cheese that has a sweet milky flavour with underlying notes of yeast. It is best to cut the rind off this cheese as, when melted, it tends to lend an unwanted bitterness to the dish.

### Fresh mozzarella
**Australia and Italy**

Mozzarella, with its silky texture and gentle sweet flavours, is the perfect cheese for a grilled cheese combination, where it lends an incredible stringiness and viscous texture without dominating flavours.

### Burrata
**Australia and Italy**

Like a pimped-out mozzarella, burrata is a stretched-curd cheese with a filling of cream and mozzarella. It will increase the richness of your melt with its unctuous interior and is best used in grilled cheese sandwiches that require minimal toasting, due to its high moisture content and quick melting. This is a luxurious alternative to mozzarella for the flatbreads on page 118, and my cheese on toast on page 64, and is also great in salads.

### Meredith marinated goat's cheese
**Victoria, Australia**

This is a kitchen staple in many homes in Australia, and for good reason. This delicious marinated soft cheese from Meredith Dairy is flavoured with herbs and a touch of garlic. Its dense texture and soft nature melts well and lends a herbaceous and slightly citrus flavour to your melt.

### Monterey Jack
**Wisconsin, USA**

The famous 'burger cheese' of the States, Monterey Jack is a semi-soft cheese with a perfect pH for melting, resulting in a uniform texture and stringiness. This cheese has a slight sweet lactic flavour but it is best utilised for its perfect melting capabilities and paired with bigger flavours.

### Roquefort
**Roquefort-sur-Soulzon, France**

This raw sheep's milk blue, with its incredibly strong blue notes, is an amazing cheese to melt. With its fragile melt-in-the-mouth texture and lingering blue spice, melted Roquefort is the perfect accompaniment to grilled steak and is good contrasted with fruit spreads.

### Manchego
**La Mancha, Spain**

La Mancha is a barren terrain and the Manchega sheep is a sturdy creature, and this terroir reflects in the flavour and texture of Spain's most popular cheese. Manchego is dry with a robust and spicy flavour that is best melted in a tapas-style grilled dish, or paired with marinated anchovies and paprika for a sensory delight like no other.

### Brie
**Australia and France**

There are many styles of brie, but the best to use in a melt are the traditional bries of France with their unctuous texture and flavours reminiscent of cauliflower and garlic.

### Camembert
**Normandy, France**

Search for a camembert from Normandy and you will not be disappointed! With its fat-glistened appearance, bulging texture, and flavours of charcuterie, cauliflower and cabbage, camembert is the best melting white mould cheese as its flavours intensify when melted. Try it with mushrooms and thyme for an incredible sensory moment. It can be used in place of brie.

# Things to know.

**Arbequina olive oil**
Highly aromatic olives are used to produce this fruity, multi-purpose olive oil from Catalonia in Spain.

**Jamón ibérico de bellota**
Cured ham from the black Iberian pig, which has been fed on acorns. The black hoof is left on during the curing process, which distinguishes it from jamón serrano.

**Korean fermented chilli paste (gochujang)**
A savoury and spicy, pungent, fermented chilli paste used in Korean cuisine, especially in the production of kimchi.

**Microplaning**
A microplane is an essential tool in my kitchen, both at home and at work. I find a cheese grater too clumsy for some jobs, while microplanes are perfect for fine grating and for grating to finish a dish.

**Muscovado sugar**
An unrefined brown sugar with a strong molasses flavour and characteristics.

**Salt flakes**
When using salt to finish a dish, I prefer to use delicate Murray River pink salt flakes. The flavour is not too strong and the flakes are soft and give great texture. However, you can use any brand of salt flakes, but please remember that they all have varying levels of salinity, so use them according to your own personal taste.

**Sorrel**
A tangy and acidic perennial herb used in salads and garnishes.

**Sriracha**
A type of hot sauce made from chilli, vinegar, sugar, garlic and salt. It can be found in specialty ingredient stores and some supermarkets.

# Finding things.

# Thank you.

*FOR BEING A FRIEND...*

I would love to thank the following people for making this book – or dream, really – a reality:

Mum and Dad (Shirley and Don) for giving me cheese, bread and a grill to help me realise this dream; my wife, Cath, for her dedication to trying out these creations and for all of the recipes I have stolen from her for this book; my sister Emma, Quin and Hannah.

Cheesemonger Anthony Femia at Maker & Monger for supplying all the cheese used in this book. Anthony also provided the cheese notes as well as expert tips on grilling, melting, storage and general cheese advice. You are a star, mate – thank you so much. Your toasted sandwiches are still the benchmark.

Michael and Pippa James at Tivoli Road, who make the BEST bread and brioche, thank you so much for providing the bread for this book. I appreciate all of the help and support.

Gary McBean and the team at Gary's Quality Meats at Prahran Market – thank you for the amazing service, produce and care. All of the meats used in this book were supplied by Gary, including the incredible Cape Grim brisket in the Reuben, the Flinders Island lamb shoulder, as well as bacon, ham, prosciutto and jamón.

I would like to thank Jane Willson for her support of this project, and the rest of the best at Hardie Grant: Mr Mark Campbell, Marg Bowman, Ariana Klepac, Susie Ashworth, Megan Ellis and Max McMaster. Thanks also to Brendan and Natalie Homan for photography and styling.

**#teamdarrenpurchese**
@almondmeal @sugarflorist @melonqueen @simondocherty1 @duyed @wclliao @cj_communications

**Suppliers and partners**
Duncan Black and David Van Rooy – Van Rooy Machinery; KitchenAid Australia – all mixing machines were supplied – thank you Feliz; Nespresso Australia.

**Special thanks**
Shannon Bennett for the foreword, support and inspiration.

Thank you to all of my supporters.

A pastry chef with a sweet tooth and a flair for culinary theatrics Darren Purchese may be, but from an early age he has made a mean cheese on toast – and still does – as *Chefs Eat Toasties Too* so scrumptiously attests. When he is not hard at work with his wife Cath at Burch & Purchese Sweet Studio in Melbourne's Chapel Street, or appearing on *MasterChef*, Darren can often be found at home in the kitchen whipping up a gastronomic treat from the simplest of meals, the not-always-so-humble toastie.

**Share your toasty creations with the world.**

*Chefs Eat Toasties Too* is on Instagram, Facebook and Twitter. Make something from this book, or create your own outrageous toastie, take a photo or video of it, upload it to one of our accounts and use the #chefseattoasties hashtag and we'll share and repost you. Get grilling!

Instagram: @ChefsEat

Twitter: @ChefsEatBooks

Facebook: @ChefsEatBooks

This edition published in 2018 by Hardie Grant Books,
an imprint of Hardie Grant Publishing
First published in 2017 as Chefs Eat Toasties Too

Hardie Grant Books (Melbourne)
Building 1, 658 Church Street
Richmond, Victoria 3121

Hardie Grant Books (London)
5th & 6th Floors
52–54 Southwark Street
London SE1 1UN

hardiegrantbooks.com

A catalogue record for this
book is available from the
National Library of Australia

Chefs Eat Melts Too
ISBN 978 1 74379 459 3

Publishing Director: Jane Willson
Managing Editor: Marg Bowman
Editor: Ariana Klepac
Designer: Mark Campbell
Typesetter: Megan Ellis
Photographer: Brendan Homan
Stylist: Natalie Homan
Proofreader: Susie Ashworth
Indexer: Max McMaster
Production Manager: Todd Rechner
Production Coordinator: Tessa Spring

Colour reproduction by Splitting Image Colour Studio
Printed in China by 1010 Printing International Limited

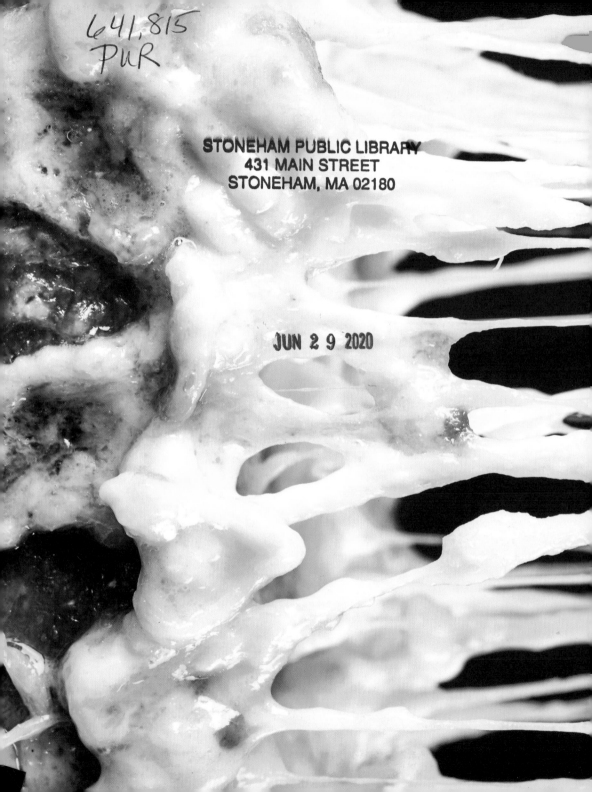